SMOKE RINGS
RISING

SMOKE RINGS RISING

Triumph of a Drug-Endangered Daughter

A Memoir

JENNIFER L. HUNT

SMOKE RINGS MEDIA, LLC

AUTHOR'S NOTE

This book has been 35 years in the making. It is a work of non-fiction, with certain names having been changed to protect friends' and family members' privacy.

Smoke Rings Media, LLC
P.O. Box 715
Oroville, CA 95965

Published 2019
Editor: Alice Peck
Editor at Large: Curt Pesmen
Cover Design: Duane Stapp, Jennifer Hunt
Book Design: Duane Stapp
Author Photo: Dean Gurr
Photographs: Getty Images, courtesy of Author
Content Production: Curt Pesmen, BoCo Media, LLC
Printed in the USA
Library of Congress Cataloging in Publication Data TXu 1-966-747
ISBN Paperback: 9780692040515
ISBN eBook: 9780692040522

CONTENTS

For my family...so history will stop repeating.

To him that will, ways are not wanting.
—George Herbert

————————

Jenny, 1973

CHAPTER ONE

SLAMMED

"Mom, I'd like to meet my father..."

T he inside of our trailer reeked of cigarette smoke and Mexican dirt weed, not the skunk that would draw in my family crowd. It was 1986, I was fourteen, and we were renting a single-wide in Concow, California—the sticks. *The Young and the Restless* theme song echoed from our nineteen-inch black-and-white TV, with a clothes hanger bent into rabbit-ears. It sat atop our inoperable color console. I'd waited days for the right moment, a safe window, where I wouldn't hurt my mother, Bobbi, with a request to meet my absent father.

I stepped from my bedroom into the living room to find Mom wearing the forearm-length jersey she wore when she needed to cover the tracks on her arms. She hid her meth use well, but I knew when she was wired. I *always* knew. As was often the case, she had a cigarette burning in the ashtray and was toking on a joint. Usually, she'd follow her soaps while reading, especially Stephen King or Dean Koontz thrillers, or writing chil-

1

dren's stories. "Corky the Cockroach," her proudest work, was about a roach that watched the goings on of a household—maybe ours! The day I inquired about my absent father, Mom was "speedily" completing a crossword puzzle.

I sat perched on the couch nearest to where she sat in her chair. In cutoffs, I had to position myself carefully to avoid being poked by the jagged edges of the vinyl covering—a telltale sign Billy Jack, my stepdad, sat there all too often. I patiently watched her complete her puzzle. As she took a hit from her joint, inhaled the marijuana, held, and then exhaled, one by one, her small, precisely rounded smoke rings drifted up to form large, indistinct ones before dissipating high into the air. Just when my courage was about to pass, *The Young and the Restless* recap revealed Ashley Abbott learning that her real father wasn't John Abbott, but, in fact, Brent Davis. Finally, I found my nerve:

"Mom, I'd like to meet my father."

"You mean Willy?"

"Yeah."

"Someday I'll have to tell you about that."

"Huh?"

In a voice excited to fill me in on our very own soap-opera saga, she let loose:

"Willy is not your real father. He loved you like you were his, though, and he treated you as if you were his own. He was so proud of you. He'd take you to the bar and show you off to everybody....Your real father's name is Ivan. He tried to say you weren't his and made me take a DNA test....Right before I was pregnant with you, I had an abortion because I did too many drugs. With you, I only did mini-bennies and marijuana....At seven months I went into labor. When I asked your father to take me to the hospital, he told me to call a cab. A cab driver picked me up, then waited at the hospital until you were born. You were five pounds even, a preemie, and had a hole in your heart....Your Grandpa Wayne was so mad you were born out of wedlock that he wouldn't even look at you in your crib....When you were six months old, you stayed with my best friend Janice while I spent six months in jail for possession of marijuana....At two years old, we ran into Ivan in a store, but you didn't know who he was....When you were five years old, someone wanted to buy you from me, but I said no. It all started when I was given that first bennie; I didn't smoke my first joint until the year you were born. I am manic-depressive."

Pummeled by my mother's shocking revelations—and her delivery—I returned to the safety of my bedroom, where I stayed for two days. Mom brought me food during mealtimes as well as a five-page handwritten confession, explanation, or apology—I'm still not sure what it was. In part, she wrote:

Jenny, I loved your father so much. I was crazy about him. His family was something that I had never seen, though. They were tight-knit; stuck together like dogs when they screwed. His sister would make up lies like I didn't watch you very well, or that I had let you roll off the bed. They all talked behind my back. I was an outsider to them. They tried to say you weren't his. I was so naive. I was young. There was no way I could have stood up to them. Jenny, I loved you so much. You were everything to me. You were all I had.

Holed up in my room, I retraced my childhood and tried piecing it together. I knew nothing of Ivan, but I had a photograph of a tall, slender man who was supposed to be my father. He stood next to a bridge holding a can of beer and wore a pair of jeans with a belt buckle set to his right. His long, shaggy hair flowed out from under his cowboy hat. That was Willy, and that picture was all I had except for two vague memories. The first was of him spanking me as a toddler during the entire walk from our car to the house because I wanted to get out on my mom's side and not his. The second was of the time I fell asleep in the very back of our station wagon atop his black leather jacket—with bubblegum in my mouth. He was just short of irate when he found out I had ruined his coat.

In my room, childhood scenes involving Mom played in my head: the fights I'd witnessed her having with different men and the explanations afterward; her partying; and myself as a toddler screaming bloody murder when she handed me off to somebody as she made her way through gigantic mahogany courtroom doors. I thought about the times she spoke of "Jenny's dad." Like, "Jenny used to sit and whittle with her dad" or "Jenny's dad used to come home and cut my nightgown off me; I'd have to hold her so he would stop." Was "Jenny's dad" Ivan or Willy? And which one was it again who told her to call a cab when she went into labor with me? Figuring out who did what, when, where, and why seemed impossible; and the more I tried to understand how my mother could lie to me about something so significant—the identity of my father—the angrier I became.

CHAPTER TWO

GOOD LITTLE GIRLS GO TO HEAVEN; BAD LITTLE GIRLS GO EVERYWHERE

Mom is another word for love...

My mother Barbara, or Bobbi, was born in California to Wayne and Maggie Osbin after Grandpa returned from his service in World War II. It was 1947, during the baby boom. She had one sister, Jeannie, who had been born in Oklahoma in 1942 before our family migrated west, landing in Stockton, CA.

Mom was a dark-haired, green-eyed beauty, and Grandma made all her clothes, including a poodle skirt that Mom used to brag to me about. That dark-haired, green-eyed beauty turned into a hard-to-handle teenager. Mom didn't talk much about her high school years, but she did say she'd sneak out of the house at night and Grandma would always cover for her, because if Grandpa had found out, Mom would have been in deep trouble. She also said that's when the Regents' song "Barbara Ann" came out, and her classmates teased her because her name was Barbara Ann, too.

Mom had dreamt of becoming an architect or writer, but at sixteen she dropped out of school and married Stanley Seifert. That was 1963. By the time she was twenty, they had two girls—Teresa and Lori—and a boy, Brian. Soon after the birth of Brian, their marriage fell apart. During their lengthy divorce, Mom signed up for welfare and she and my siblings moved in with my grandparents. Stanley sought custody of Brian, but not Teresa or Lori. Mom said he tricked her by telling her the wrong court date for a hearing and won by default.

Mom had a wayward tendency about her, and given her lack of stability, when she moved out of Grandma and Grandpa's, Teresa and Lori, around six and five at the time, stayed behind. While separated from Stanley, Mom had a brief relationship with another man and became pregnant with me. I was born in 1971. Since she was technically still married, I share my last name with her and my siblings—Seifert. I was six months old when her divorce from Stanley was final.

Much later in Mom's life, she would shake her head and wonder out loud why she divorced Stanley. "He was a good provider. I had a nice home. I always had nice things. I would shop from *Spiegel.* He just would always go around smelling everything, and that drove me crazy!"

I'd think, *But, Mom, then I wouldn't be here!*

Grandma Maggie and Grandpa Wayne, indeed part of The Greatest Generation, were my only exposure to how a traditional family looked and acted. Grandpa had his own carpenter/handyman business; Grandma was a cook at the San Joaquin County General Hospital, which is where I was born.

Grandpa, a pastor's son, was set in his ways. To me, he was an unapproachable man who never smiled. That, of course, made me curious about him, but he didn't give me the time of day. He was always busy sanding, painting, grinding, or building something simply because he could. Everything he worked on was amazing. One morning, as a toddler, I was "investigating" one of his projects: two sawhorses with planks across them and an open gallon container of whitewash. The next thing I knew, paint was everywhere—all over me, all over the boards, and all over the grass. I feared what Grandpa was going to do to me. Mom came running when she heard my hysterical cry. I got a bath, but no word from Grandpa. Later, when I was on the living room floor watching *Mighty Mouse,* he came in and sat in his recliner, which was *his* spot, next to his chewing tobacco spittoon.

"Grandpa, Mighty Mouse is my hero!"

"Quiet!" he yelled as he changed the station to the news.

Another time, I heard a commotion in the backyard, so I ran out to the porch to see what was going on. Grandpa yelled again, this time, "Get back in the house!" as he sprayed his dog Bozo and a female apart with the hose. His tone sent a shiver down my spine; I hurried inside.

Grandma, however, was solid gold, second only to Mom. She was loving and kind. Plus, she always kept Bubble Yum in her purse for me to find. Many of my memories of her involve wonderful meals. For breakfast, she'd prepare biscuits filled with homemade jam and the best country gravy ever, or my favorite: her perfectly shaped Mickey Mouse pancakes. When I'd opt for cereal instead, she'd serve it with hot buttered toast that I'd dip into cold whole milk. By afternoon, as dinner was going into the oven, a treat would be cooling on the counter: a juicy, sweet peach cobbler or the newest cake recipe she just had to try.

Outside of being a great cook, Grandma was also a saver, in more ways than one. When I'd taunt "Red," her Rhode Island Red rooster, by lunging at him on my tricycle until he was flogging mad, she was always there to rescue me—thank goodness, because he was big. And as for being frugal, she loved visiting yard sales and occasionally would take me with her. One afternoon in early summer, I found a beautiful rectangular plaque with a tiny red rose on it. It read: *Mom is another word for love.* Grandma gave me the dime to pay for it, and I took it home and gave it to my mother. I still remember the look on her face as she accepted it. No matter where we lived, that plaque rested on top of her bedroom dresser.

As a child, my favorite place to be was wherever Mom was, but my happiest was at Grandma's, especially when Teresa and Lori were home. It had never been a secret that I had a different father than they did, it was obvious: they were tall, blond-haired, and blue-eyed, while I was short, brown-haired, and brown-eyed. In addition, I once called their father "Dad," and they gave me a stern look that told me otherwise. None of the biological stuff mattered, though; seven and six years older, they were my big sisters, I was their "Fer"—short for Jennifer—and there was always fun to be had with the blond-haired, blue-eyed hellions.

At Grandma's, Teresa and Lori would open the wooden turntable, toss on some vinyl, and sing along with—and gawk at—Shaun Cassidy and Leif Garrett. The three of us danced "The Hustle" across the living room floor. We'd play "I Dropped My Dolly in the Dirt," "Jesus Loves Me," and the "Heart and Soul" duet on the piano. Without them, I'd happily sing along with *Sesame Street*, "Three of these kids belong together; three of these kids are kind of the same; but one of these kids is doing his own thing..." I loved and looked up to my sisters, but I knew at a very early age I was part them, but also part "me" and I liked doing my own thing—except that time I followed their lead and we all shoplifted from the corner store.

Just down the street from Grandma's house was a market. While the three of us were inside, my sisters stole some candy and I stole a pacifier. (I know, I know. At about four, I *was* practically a baby.) Walking back to Grandma's, with the stolen pacifier in my mouth, I thought I was just as cool as they were. They laughed at me while eating their candy. Back at the house, Mom looked at me as if to ask, *"Where in the world did you get a pacifier?"*

I had a few good friends who lived near Grandma's—Tommy, Pumpkin, and Peanut—and one foe: Joey. I didn't like Joey because he always messed with my things, like my plastic Hawaiian lei that I left in Mom's car. One afternoon I found its petals strewn all over the back seat and floorboard. Joey was the only one besides me who had been in the car around that time. His new plastic gun lay there unharmed. Fuming mad, I grabbed it and stuck it under the front of Mom's rear tire. When she took off—*crunch!* She stopped and stepped out of the car to see what the noise was. When she figured it out, she glanced over at me. I sensed she found my satisfaction in its destruction humorous. I later told Joey what happened to his gun; he never messed with my things again.

———

Life at Grandma's was entirely different from with Mom, who once told me she felt like my grandparents had raised her in a bubble, and it had made her naïve. I gather that's why when it came to child rearing, she took the opposite approach: no censoring, period. With Mom, rather than waking up to the sweet smell of home cooking, sometimes I'd wake up to the bed bouncing as she was getting it on with someone. Rather than passing me a Mickey Mouse pancake, Mom would pass me a joint. Once she gave me a burning roach, and I crawled into the fort I made under our kitchen table with it and fell asleep. Another time, I woke up in a smoke-filled room, unable to breathe: an unsettling memory that surfaced when I was an adult.

More her sidekick than her kid, I tagged along *everywhere*—and preferred it that way—through the 1970s with our free-spirited, substance-using mother. Because of my unfiltered exposure, Mom never knew what to expect out of my mouth. Like the time when she got back into our car after using the payphone outside of the adult bookstore. Proud that I had figured out the word written on the window, I said, "Mom, I know how to spell sex, S-E-X." She just chuckled. Or, after overhearing her tell my sisters that the Hartleys—our family friends—fed their dog acid, I asked, "Mom, what does acid look like?" That one left her speechless.

The (pharmaceutical) lingo around our excursions ran the gamut from uppers—black beauties, Christmas trees, and bennies—to downers—green monsters, yellow jackets, and reds, which to some were ruby slippers. Mom always laughed when she told people, "Jenny had a doll named Ruby that had only one eye. She'd tote her everywhere." Until I was grown, I thought she laughed because Ruby had only one eye.

Mom liked to party, and one gathering she took me to was at a huge white house that was supposedly owned by someone related to Jim Nabors of *Gomer Pyle* fame. Mom and I took a tour of the inside of the near-mansion. The master bedroom had a heart-shaped waterbed covered with a red velvet blanket tucked in neatly. In the backyard was a built-in swimming pool, which was great since I was just learning to swim.

Seated comfortably in a chair by the pool, Mom chatted with a group of people as I paced the deck, eager to hop into the water, but I couldn't find the courage to do so. Suddenly, some guy did it for me—right into the deep end. In a panic, I doggy-paddled as fast as I could to stay afloat. Realizing I could barely swim, someone helped me out of the pool. Not making a big deal about it, Mom simply walked me to where she had been sitting. After crying, I pouted, keeping the fool who pushed me in sight.

After my pouting wore off, I got up and went to use the restroom. When I was finished, I snooped around and noticed a mirror with white lines and a razor blade on top of the clothes dryer. Wondering whether the razor was sharp, I tested it on my left index finger. It was. Mom came to my rescue as I cried and bled. I didn't get in any trouble, but I still do have the scar.

I don't remember Mom ever yelling or disciplining me. When she got mad, a "Jennifer Michelle" (Michelle wasn't even my middle name) was enough for me to know I had crossed the line.

Mom brought me along to over- or late-night parties—sometimes at strangers' houses—where she'd find a place for me to sleep. Resting on someone's couch one evening, I heard for the first time what became my favorite childhood song: Paul Anka's "Put Your Head on my Shoulder." Although I had no idea who Paul was, I spent many days dreaming of him singing that song solely to me.

The years I turned five and six must have been busy ones for Mom. According to a handwritten date on the back of a picture I have of her and Philip—one of her several husbands—standing before an officiant holding a Bible, they married in 1976. Philip had oily, dark hair, and he drank incessantly. I have only two memories of Mom's time with this man: a crab feed in Oregon with his family and a camping trip. At the crab feed, Mom had passed out in a bedroom. Sitting at the foot of the bed, I was pinching her toes with the pinchers from the crabs. She would stir, look up at me, and then go right back to sleep. During the camping trip, she and Philip fought. I watched my mom pick up the biggest rock I could ever imagine a 145-pound woman lifting and throw it at him with every intention of inflicting pain. Their marriage was brief, and the only proof I can find of it is that photograph, but Mom kept his last name, Yoakum, for decades.

After Philip, my sisters began spending more time with Mom and me. This just added to the adventure. Mom would drive, Teresa would rest in the passenger seat with her leathery feet (from being barefoot) hanging out the window, Lori would ride in the center with her feet on the dash, often singing Janis Joplin's "Mercedes Benz" or Wayne Cochran's "Last Kiss," and I would have the backseat all to myself. That was the way we rolled all through Okieville aka Stockton, California. Anytime we had to stop for a train at a railroad crossing, my sisters would jump out of our car and run around it as many times as they could until the *ding, ding, ding* signaled us to drive on, and then they'd jump back in. People in other cars would either glare or smile; I just watched my sisters and thought how great they were.

The four of us would go dumpster diving. Mom was privy to the days of the week that her favorite thrift stores threw out dated merchandise. She, my sisters, and I would climb in over the sides of the gondolas behind the secondhand shops and sort through the refuse that, on a good day, was piled up half the height of the bin. We'd come home with lots of prize finds— purses, shoes, hats, and toys.

At the movie theater, ratings didn't matter. As we all stood in line to see *The Exorcist* the year it came out—I was five—Teresa voiced her concern saying, "Mom, the sign says you have to be seventeen."

Mom's response? "Oh, it's okay."

I watched *The Exorcist* in the front row with my hands over my face, occasionally peeking through my fingers during a safe moment. It was the same with *The Amityville Horror*. It's no wonder I bathed with my dog next to the tub until I was a teenager.

The shows we saw at the cinema weren't all scary. Seated with my sisters in the very back row, we watched the first *Rocky* film. I was glued to the screen. Fighting with heart, no matter how many times the Italian Stallion got knocked down in the ring, he eventually rose again. *"Adrian!"*

I was the (self-appointed) joint roller of my family. I couldn't yet tie my shoes, but I could roll you a doobie and/or fix you up a "cocktail" cigarette by removing a tiny bit of tobacco from the end, packing it lightly with a roach, and gently twisting the tip. At home, I'd practice. First, I'd separate the marijuana from the seeds. Using a playing card, I'd sweep it up a slightly tilted tray, and the seeds would tumble to the bottom. (A joint smoked with seeds popped like a low-grade firecracker.) Then, while watching cartoons, I'd practice my craft, finishing the job off by gently licking the glue edge of the Zig-Zag paper to hold it, somewhat, together.

When my family and I took road trips, one of my sisters in the front seat would pass the tray with the pot, papers, and the rolling machine to me in the back. They knew I enjoyed doing it. Using the roller, I could make a joint look better. When I was finished, I'd hand the joint and setup over to the front, then lie down and bury my head in the dark crack where the seat bottom met the back. I'd dream or nap until we got wherever we were going.

It was just my mom and me when we went to Louisiana. She had a boyfriend employed by an offshore drilling outfit there. Traveling through New Orleans at night, she pulled over to pick up two male teenage-looking hitchhikers. One was taller and leaner than the other. Both wore jackets, as it was chilly outside. I was in the front seat, so they hopped into the back. On the way to wherever we were going, Mom pulled into a grocery store's parking lot. She and I got out of the car and walked toward the entrance of the market. About halfway there, she realized she had left her car keys in the ignition.

"Jenny," she suggested, "why don't you go and wait in the car while I run into the store?"

"No," I said, knowing even at my young age the absurdity of her request.

We made our way through the market as my tipsy mom searched specifically for a bottle of cheap wine called "Tickle Pink." I'll never forget: after she found it, on our way to the checkout, she dropped the bottle. It shattered all over the floor of the main aisle of the grocery store. We stood next to the pink puddle until an employee came to clean up her mess. Unfazed, Mom purchased a replacement bottle, and we exited the store. Then we had to find the car. It's hard to find your car in the daylight and sober, let alone in the dark and inebriated, and especially when it isn't there.

Thankful that I'd had the wits to not go back and wait in that car with those boys, I watched Mom on the payphone calling my grandma and grandpa for help. Grandma always helped, this time with bus tickets. Mom and I boarded a Greyhound to California. Among the passengers, I'm told, were members of the band Blood, Sweat, and Tears, who played music—and partied—for much of our journey back home to the Golden State.

The police didn't find the boys, but they did find our car. It had been dumped under a bridge into a canal.

Around that time, Mom had yet another boyfriend. This one lived in Indio, California. He didn't like me, and I didn't like him—or his two-year-old twit of a son. It was a busy house with my sisters there, too. I sure don't remember that boyfriend's name, but he had a poodle I'll never forget. My sisters and I had tie-dyed some T-shirts in the bathtub by twisting them tight, securing them with rubber bands, and submerging them under the colored water. Mom's boyfriend used some of the dye and dyed the dog bright, bright lime green. I couldn't believe it—it practically glowed.

One morning while in Indio, Lori made French toast, bacon and eggs, and orange juice for breakfast. When it was finished, she helped me set up plates for Mom and the boyfriend. I was going to surprise them with breakfast in bed. I had Mom's plate in both hands, and I walked to her bedroom door. I must not have knocked, but I managed to turn the knob and open the door slightly. The boyfriend was on top of Mom. Apparently, I had interrupted him. He fiercely yelled, "Get out!" I stepped back and closed the door. A couple of days later, I got my revenge: while he and Mom were sleeping, I painted his twit son's fingernails pink. The boyfriend was not happy about it and gave me a good chewing. It was worth it.

Mom hadn't done anything when he yelled at me, but in a matter of days he was history. She, my sisters, and I gathered all our laundry into bags and hampers, and we loaded everything into the trunk of our car. Mom told the boyfriend that we were going to the Laundromat, but the truth was she was leaving him. We didn't make it very far, though, because we ended up with a flat tire on the freeway. Cars and trucks passed us like we weren't there. My sisters and I sat on the trunk of the car and we'd gesture our fists up and down for the big rigs to blow their horns. They would honk and smile as they drove by. Finally, a man in a pickup truck with an attached apple cart of sorts stopped. He gave each of us girls an apple, some water, and helped Mom get the spare tire on. Soon we were on our way back to Okieville, away from the boyfriend.

Back in Stockton, Mom and my sisters, barely twelve and thirteen by this time, would regularly visit Dr. Weiss, our family doctor. He had delivered Mom when she was born. Teresa and Lori were both a little on the heavy side, but Mom wasn't. All three of them would gear up inside the car in the parking lot before their appointment by strapping ankle weights underneath their bell-bottoms. Then, they would go into his office to be weighed. One by one, as each stood on the scale, Dr. Weiss would say, "Oh, you're just a little bit overweight." He'd send them out with diet pills that Mom called "Upjohns"—speed. They would sit in the car, still in the parking lot, and Mom would scrape the outer coating of the pink pills off over a mirror. I wasn't privy to what she (or they) did with them afterward, because, sensing it was none of my business, I'd sink deep into the backseat to give them privacy. According to Teresa years later, Mom, who resembled her older sister Jeannie, would also obtain Upjohns from a Dr. Fujimori's office. She would get all gussied up one day and go in for her appointment as herself, then go in the next day without makeup as her sister. Teresa said Mom sold many of the pills.

————

I started kindergarten at Elmwood Elementary School in 1977. Elmwood was my first glimpse of structure. Every activity involved a single-file line—the drinking fountain, the lunch room, the playground, and entering and leaving the classroom. I loved school, and my teacher, Mrs. Meyn. At a parent-teacher conference, she told Mom, "Jenny does everything I ask her to do, then will sit and put her head down on her desk without being told." Mom looked at me in a strange way, as if I knew how to behave after all. When the conference was over, sounding a bit surprised, maybe confused, Mom told me, "Your teacher said that, with a little support, you're capable of doing anything you want to in this world." I think that was Mrs. Meyn's way of telling my mom to step it up a little.

Right before Thanksgiving of that same year, my maternal Great-Grandpa Riley died, so in a matter of months, Grandma Maggie and Grandpa Wayne moved from their home—my happiest place—into Great-Granny Sarah's house a few miles away to take care of her. Teresa and Lori moved in with our family friends, the Hartleys.

In no time, I came to love Great-Granny's home, too. It was furnished with dark wooden antiques, including claw-foot tables. The kitchen was decorated in everything strawberry, even white carpet with strawberry vines. Atop the hutch sat a black rotary phone, and I can still recall the number. On Grandma Maggie's deep purple bedroom wall hung another wood-encased phone for looks. Grandma never went to church or spoke of Jesus or God, but also in her room, next to her light switch, was a picture of Him. If you stood a couple feet away from it and looked closely, Jesus' eyes would be closed. If you closed your eyes, stepped back, counted to ten, then opened your eyes, His eyes would be open. Given I was afraid of ghosts, it always freaked me out.

Grandma Maggie and Great-Granny Sarah loved to watch their "stories," or soaps operas. I liked to memorize all the catchy commercials: "444-5555, that's the number to the Classified," in particular. After the daytime shows, Grandma often put on music: Loretta Lynn, Charley Pride, or Merle Haggard. Ironically, "Okie from Muskogee" seemed to always be playing when my sisters, struck with the marijuana munchies, were raiding the refrigerator.

Great-Granny's house came to be my "safe" place, and I received the second spanking of my life when I ran there for protection. The day had started out at the park with Mom and a group of her friends. Playing in the playground, I noticed voices becoming elevated between a man and a woman within Mom's group. I guess they could have been kidding around, but I thought a fight was about to break out. I grew afraid and got disoriented in the park, but found an exit, an exit that led back to Great-Granny's house. I had traveled four or five blocks. Mom and her friends frantically searched for me, and eventually found me there. I got my spanking as Mom firmly told me, "Don't you ever do that again!"

Right before Christmas of 1978, the same year my grandparents moved into Great-Granny Sarah's, Grandpa Wayne died suddenly of a heart attack. He was just sixty-two. Bozo, his beloved dog, passed away right after. It had to have been hard on Grandma losing her father and husband so closely in time, but aside from at Grandpa Wayne's funeral, I never saw her cry over either. Instead, unwavering, Grandma stood strong. Although the holidays had been hard on us, they were always special at Great-Granny Sarah's. Each Thanksgiving, our extended family came together for a turkey feast that included Grandma Maggie's homemade cornbread stuffing and her famous fruit salad. Christmas was the same, except we had a ham dinner and her colorful fruitcake, followed by unwrapping presents in front of an elaborately decorated tree with a cardinal bird ornament that sang endlessly.

Without Grandpa, Grandma was left to look after the family. She disagreed with Mom's lifestyle and, being the caretaker that she was, often tried to convince me to move in with her. Once she said she'd put my hair up in pigtails every single day if only I would. I never wanted to, though, not even for pigtails. Being with Mom was much more interesting. Grandma may have been opposed to Mom's way of life, but I never heard her complain about it. Instead, she'd secretly hand her a twenty-dollar bill and whisper, "Don't let Granny know."

CHAPTER THREE

SOLOMON'S PLEASURE

As with all of her previous relationships with men, Mom seemed happy in the beginning of hers with Junior, too...

I'd always thought Mom had five husbands, but now I can only count four. She married Stanley, Philip, Junior, and after eighteen years together and a good cry on my back porch about how he always cheated on her, she also married Billy Jack.

At seven years old, I waited in the van while Mom and Junior (whose given name was Solomon) ran into City Hall to wed. Junior had thin, dark, greasy, shoulder-length hair and worked at a company that made large plastic signs for businesses—something you might see on the façade of Target or Macy's. Grandma and Grandpa's previous home was just around the corner from our new one with Junior, and I passed Great-Granny's on my walk to and from school. Location-wise, our house was perfect, but it was creepy and I believed haunted. Napping one day in Mom and Junior's room, I swear I heard the floor creaking with footsteps walking around me. Paralyzed with fear, I stayed flat on the bed until Mom came in much later. I didn't sleep in their room after that, just snooped. When a tiny Buddha figurine appeared next to the "Mom is Another Word for Love" plaque on their dresser, I asked Mom about it. She said rubbing his belly would bring good luck. Thinking that was cool, I sometimes carried him in my sweatshirt pocket, often stroking his midsection.

As with all of her previous relationships with men, Mom seemed happy in the beginning of hers with Junior, too—going so far as to get "JR" tattooed on one of her breasts and "Solomon's Pleasure" on the back of her right shoulder—but it wasn't long before they were fighting. And often. I'd sit crouched up next to their bedroom door and hear them scream, yell, and hit. Later, I'd hear the stories of how Junior had a gun or knife, how they had wrestled over it, and how Mom had told him, "Just use it, motherfucker!" I wasn't sure if she was telling him to use it on himself or on her. I also heard her tell someone that the only way she could avoid a fight with him was to be "screwed" every night.

Mom was extremely sad while she was with Junior—even when there was a joint between her fingers. Trying to make her happy, I'd cater to her the best I could. I'd write phonetic notes telling how much I loved her. I'd even play jokes on her, at the most unsuspecting moments. Like the time she walked into my room to put away some clean clothes. I was playing with Ken and Barbie. Mom startled me because Ken and Barbie were doing the nasty. As the door opened wide and she came inside, in my

The Amityville Horror scary voice, I let out a bloodcurdling, "Get out." She stood frozen. Her heart may have even stopped beating for a second. I couldn't stop laughing. When I did, I nonchalantly asked, "Mom, what religion are we?"

With a quizzical look and a chuckle, "Christian. Why?"

"Oh, I don't know. Just wondering. Are ghosts real?"

"Yes, but they can't hurt you. They can only scare you to make you hurt yourself."

"Oh."

I would forget about the unhappiness in my home when I was at Tommy's or Brandy's house. Tommy, my friend since Grandma and Grandpa had resided in their original home, lived across the street from me, beyond the parking lot of the vacant building on the corner. One day we were taking turns jumping from stacked pallets over a hog-wire fence that separated his yard from that parking lot. We were having fun until I jumped over and he didn't wait for me to get out of the way. When he landed, he knocked the wind out of me. In a panic, I ran home to Mom. Tommy's mother sent him over to apologize. I wasn't mad; I knew it was an accident. I could tell he felt badly. But then, my mom told me to go over to Tommy's and apologize back.

"Why?" I asked. "He's the one who jumped on me."

"Because," she said. "Be the bigger person."

She always said that: "Be the bigger person. Be the bigger person." Why did I always have to be the bigger person? As Mom directed, I walked across the lot, hopped the fence, and apologized to him for—well, I guess hurting me. I misinterpreted her lesson that day to mean that I should always put myself last, and

I carried that mindset into adulthood.

Brandy was sort of my friend, but a brat. She lived in an up-scale house on the next block. We were close in age and played together sometimes. Her parents threw her a great big party for one of her birthdays with games and all, the kind of party most kids would die for. During Pin the Tail on the Donkey, each child drew numbers to see who would go first. I drew the number one and Brandy drew fourteen. This upset Brandy, and she threw a temper tantrum as big as her party. Her mom leaned over to me and asked, "Jenny, since it's her birthday, do you mind if she goes first?" Being "the bigger person," I swapped and moved to the end of the line.

I may have given Brandy her way at her party, but I didn't forget about her taking my spot in line for Pin the Tail on the Donkey. I had a Siamese cat named Simon. He was cross-eyed, his once-broken tail was stuck at ninety degrees, and he had a long, deep meow. The next time Brandy was at my house, I asked her if she wanted to play with my Play-Doh. She said yes. I told her it was hidden in the pile of sand (cat litter) over by the fence. She said it was a bit dry but played with it anyway. I don't think she ever figured it out. I guess I didn't have it in me to *always* be the bigger person.

Teresa and Lori still lived with the Hartleys, but sometimes stayed with Junior, Mom, and me. The top bunk was mine, but there was a bottom bunk and a twin bed in my room available for them whenever they wanted. Grooming themselves in our bath-room one morning, they were talking about how some guy was "such a pervert." Bathing in the tub with Daisy Mae, my Doberman Pinscher named after Daisy Duke, by my side, I asked, "What's a pervert?" They both laughed and looked at me like they didn't know how to answer my question.

Finally, Teresa said, "It's someone who farts in the bathtub."

Lori added, "Yes! So, don't be a pervert!"

It took me years to figure out that a pervert wasn't someone who farted in the bathtub.

Teresa, the tomboy of our family, never wore makeup, just a folded bandana around her forehead. Usually in bell-bottoms and bare feet, she carried herself with a dominant gait. She came to have BTRH for "Born to Raise Hell" emblazoned across the upper fingers of her right hand and a star tattoo above her ankle.

During a brave moment, wearing her bandana, bell-bottoms, and bare feet, Teresa stood atop the Delta Canal bank straddling her ten-speed bicycle—that had only front brakes. She started downhill. When she tried to slow, she toppled over the handlebars and broke her jaw. The doctor wired her jaw shut and put her on a liquid diet. After she healed, she was the best at talking like Donald Duck, and would do it whenever I asked her to, usually at my bedtime.

One evening, bleeding profusely from her arm, Teresa came running up the street to our house. She had gotten into a fight, and a group of girls were chasing her. During the scrap, to free up her hands, Teresa threw down her Coke bottle. One of her opponents grabbed and broke it, then cut Teresa with it. "Two inches higher, and it could have hit her jugular," I heard after the fact. Teresa ran into the house. Mom used my croquet mallet to chase the girls away. They turned right back around.

Lori, the lover of the family, always wore makeup and adorned herself with all sorts of jewelry, especially turquoise. In a sexy blouse and a pair of jeans, a dress, or even shorty-shorts, she carried herself with a feminine strut. She came to have a butterfly tattooed on the back of one of her shoulders and a small rose on her left forearm. Later she had "Ladies Love Outlaws" inked across her upper back.

Lori dreamed of getting married. She wanted the whole get-up, too—the fancy wedding, the dress, the ring—but mostly a man that loved her. Neither Teresa nor Lori was anywhere near legal age, but late one evening they showed up at our house twitterpated to no end. Each had met someone with whom they were going to run away and get married—that night. A double wedding. I sat upright on my top bunk and watched them eagerly gather their belongings before going on their way. It apparently didn't pan out, however, because neither of them got hitched at that time.

At fifteen, Teresa met Rick. Soon thereafter, expecting my niece Amber, they moved into their own place. Lori and I were roller-skating from their house to the corner store one afternoon. Gracefully gliding, Lori was ahead of me in her rolled-up shorty-shorts; I was doing my best to just stay on my feet. As we approached the store, a vehicle behind us honked. Startled by the sound, I fell and slammed my head on the asphalt. I was out cold. The man who honked helped Lori get me back to Teresa's, where Mom was. When I came to, Mom said the man, a preacher, felt terrible about the accident and had knelt next to the couch and prayed over me.

———

Kindergarten at Elmwood had been great, but according to the school's records, my attendance during first grade was "poor" and second was "very poor." "Jenny's parents say she's susceptible to colds, the flu, and pneumonia," one reads. I wasn't sick; I only went to school when I wanted. If I chose to stay home, watch TV, and eat cereal all day on the couch, I could. Plus, I wore a dress to school every day that I went, and a group of girls didn't like it, especially when I'd fly across and back on the monkey bars without falling. Teasing me, they'd laugh and lie, say I wasn't wearing underwear. Staying home was an easy way to avoid them. Upon my return to school, sometimes I'd write my own absence note: "Jenny was ill." I'd wake Mom up long enough to sign it, then I'd set out to Elmwood. On my way home, I'd stop by my great-granny's for a hug and a handful of lemon drops.

My attendance in the third grade, however, picked up. That year, I remember yearning to participate in the extracurricular activities—gymnastics, swimming, dance—that some students talked about, but my only outlet was being at school, and I loved it. Each morning, I'd wake to my Raggedy Ann and Andy alarm clock:

"Andy, Andy, please get up, it's time to call our friends."
"Okay, Ann, I'm awake, let's shout it once again."
"We are here to wake you, here we are to say, 'Please get up,
brush your teeth, and start your happy day.'"

I'd get up, put on a dress, pour a bowl of cereal or make my own scrambled eggs with ketchup, then hit the road.

Freckle-faced Jimmy Speers was my first crush. He, too, was in the third grade. I'd dream of promenading to class wearing a beautiful hoopskirt dress, carrying a matching parasol, and seeing him awestruck by my presence. That dream never came true, however, because Jimmy liked a girl named Candy. I could never understand why someone would name their daughter "Candy."

The only days I missed during the third grade when not genuinely sick were when we had awards ceremonies. Perhaps I earned them, or perhaps the teacher felt my self-esteem needed a boost, but I always got awards: Student of the Week, Student of the Month, and every other one given to third graders. I missed those days because I was embarrassed that—with the whole school there—my mom might show up. I was embarrassed that she might not. I was embarrassed that my sister Teresa would come instead, in bell-bottoms and a bandana, and shout, "That's my sissy!" Mostly, I was embarrassed to be in front of a crowd. Rather, I'd accept my awards the next day in class and risk the teacher's curiosity about why I was absent.

Mom and Junior continued to fight, and Mom coped with it the only way she knew how: passed out for days on Teresa's couch. On what I presume were downers, she'd wake up only long enough to eat. It was when I was in the third grade that Lori, knowing how unhappy Mom was with Junior, introduced her to her new boyfriend Stacy's uncle, Billy Jack, who was a carny at the San Joaquin County Fair. Billy Jack came over to meet us one afternoon while Junior was at work. He brought me a large stuffed lion and a bear, the kind you win at a carnival. Billy Jack was short and stout, and he acted like a tough guy. His pudgy face reminded me of a bulldog's.

Right before Christmas, when I was nine, Mom posed the question: "Jenny, would you rather we stay here with Junior until after Christmas and have a lot of nice presents, or would you rather we leave Junior before Christmas but not have so many?"

Thoroughly aware of how she and Junior fought, I said, "Mom, I want you to be happy, so before." We packed up and off we went to a new home...again.

CHAPTER FOUR

SMOKE FOLLOWS BEAUTY

Luckily the tailpipe smoked heavily, because it covered up the marijuana scent wafting from the car when Mom opened the door...

Our move from Junior's took us outside of Okieville, but we were still in Stockton. Billy Jack never worked after that carny job, but he didn't hit or talk down to Mom, and she seemed happy. My sisters were always over, and even our brother Brian came to visit us sometimes. I was happy, too.

Billy Jack's house was a three-bedroom. When people entered, one of the first things they'd see was a velour picture of Satan on the living room wall. Billy Jack's joke was that it was to ward off "solicitors" who came knocking on our door to share the "good news." He told us that he'd greet them with it in hand and explain, "This is who we believe in." I never saw him do it, but I'm positive he would have if given the opportunity.

I had my own room. The carnival animals that Billy Jack gave me covered my neatly made, full-size bed that was opposite a window. I learned to keep the curtains adjusted appropriately once I caught Billy Jack's nephew, Mitch—apparently a pervert!—watching me change clothes. Billy Jack had many nieces and nephews, my newly acquired cousins, all of whom were older than me.

The backyard was spacious. I shot my one and only bird with a BB gun there. A blue jay, I couldn't believe I hit it—and on my first shot. As soon as it went down, however, I felt horrible. I knew I could never do that again.

Billy Jack's nickname for me became "Angel Eyes," at least for a while. I'd sit and read to him on the couch because he said he couldn't. However, he could make his way through the many *High Times* magazines around our house somehow. He set two rules for me: I had to go to school and I had to finish all the food on my dinner plate—at the table, not seated with him and Mom on the living room couch. I was okay with both. When I did something wrong, he'd jokingly tell me, "See? That's what you get for doing your own thinking." That wasn't so bad either. Shortly after moving in with Billy Jack, however, Mom gave me my third, and last, spanking. I had recently gotten my ears pierced, and my earlobes became infected. Mom took the posts out to clean them, but it was too painful for me to let her put them back in, so I threw a fit. She used a switch on me for that one. My ears are still pierced.

Billy Jack had hunting hounds in kennels in the backyard, which meant I could keep my pal, Daisy Mae. That girl looked after me. Like the night I started vomiting, and she went into Mom and Billy Jack's room and woke Mom up. I had many frayed pant legs from when Daisy and I played together. Yet one day I came home from school to find she was gone. Mom said they had to give her away to someone who could feed and take care of her better than we could. Billy Jack owned at least four hounds at any given time, so I didn't buy her story. I never did learn the truth.

Billy Jack took excellent care of his dogs and had a knack for training them. He had a caged raccoon that he'd use to teach them to "tree" with. He'd tether the "coon," as he'd call it, to a long rope. When his dogs were plenty riled up, he would release the poor creature and let the dogs chase it up the tall oak in the yard. I thought it was plain mean. Most of his dogs were obedient and well mannered, but one female wasn't. I tagged along on a hunting trip once with him and Mom. This dog wouldn't load into his pickup truck. From afar, she'd stand there and stare at us. As soon as we drove up and got near her, she'd dart off, then stop again and stare. The last time she darted ahead and stopped, Billy Jack started off in first gear, sped up and shifted to second, and ran right into her hind quarters. He got out and loaded that now-obedient bitch into the truck. I cried. Mom didn't say a word.

Mom also didn't say a word after an incident at the Laundromat, where we spent a lot of time because we didn't own a washer and dryer. I was the one who spent a lot of time, because I loved to do the laundry. Mom and Billy Jack would take off or sit out in the car and smoke pot. Later they'd tell me what a great wife I was going to make someone someday. I enjoyed the kudos. One afternoon, Billy Jack stayed in the Laundromat eying a dryer full of some man's Levi's. When our laundry had finished, Billy Jack casually loaded all the Levi's into our baskets with our clothes. Hastily, we made our way to our car. The man, in no time, figured out what happened and followed us and confronted Billy Jack. Billy Jack pulled out a knife, and the guy backed off. We drove away with his Levi's. Like Mom, I didn't say a word.

Billy Jack didn't work, but he didn't fight with Mom. They did smoke a lot of pot. And they smoked it everywhere—in the house, in the car, outside—and all the time. Marijuana was with us when we took a trip to the Grand Canyon and when we went tubing down the Mokelumne River. At the drive-in, lying in the back of our Plymouth Valiant station wagon with the tailgate open, we had our blankets, munchies, and Pepsi handy. They toked it up to Cheech and Chong's *Up in Smoke* and *The Jerk,* while I caught a contact high.

In the fourth grade, I still loved—and was allowed—to roll joints for people. I was also still allowed to smoke with my family if I wanted. Sometimes, when the cousins were over, everybody would sit under a large, clear, plastic "tent" that was more like a plastic bubble, on the living room floor and smoke inside of it. They'd invite me in: "There's nothing wrong with it; the Indians did it." Sometimes I would. I was even welcome to hit the bong, but only did so a couple of times. I wasn't a pro, but I could suck hard enough to feel the bubbles and knew when to remove my finger from the carburetor. Cousin Chad demonstrated how to smoke hash from underneath a cup once, but I don't recall partaking in it.

I liked the smell of some strains of the marijuana, especially skunk, but if ever I wanted to get away from it, it was impossible to escape. I'd move around from spot to spot, but it always meandered my way. If someone noticed my move, they would chime in, hacking and coughing if it was good weed, "Smoke follows beauty," and smile at me.

While high, people would sit around and talk about all the things they could have done in life, or what they should have done, or even what they still might do. It was all just talk. One afternoon, as if in some sort of pipe dream, Billy Jack said, "Jenny, you should become a stenographer—they make the bucks!" Everyone in the room agreed with him. I had no idea what a stenographer was. Mom chimed in: "A stenographer sits in the middle of a courtroom and types everything said down on a funny little machine." Knowing I was shy, she added, "They only have to speak when asked to read back what they typed." It sounded like a great job.

I attended August Elementary School during the fourth grade. Grandma Maggie bought me a clarinet so I could play in the band. When things were tough, Mom would hock it, but she'd usually get it out on the first of the month when her welfare check came in. I was walking home from school one day, my clarinet in hand, when two older girls closed in on me from behind. They began mocking and shoving me. When I reached my front door, I told Teresa and Lori. They stormed out of the house and caught up with those girls. My sisters didn't hurt them, just gave them a taste of their own medicine.

Teresa took care of me in her own way. Sometimes she'd sit

and brush my hair for nearly an hour at a time. I loved it when she did that because it made my entire body tingle, but she was really checking for head lice. Talking like Donald Duck, she'd pick through my hair like a mother monkey does to her young, examining anything that looked like it was an egg or had legs. Afterward, she'd do her smoke-rings trick for me. That entailed her pulling the cellophane wrapper partway down from her Marlboro pack, taking a drag from her cigarette, then burning a small hole into the base of the wrapper with the cigarette's ember. Once that was done, exhaling softly, she'd blow her drag into the hole. While holding the pack horizontally, she'd lightly tap the bottom of the wrapper, and tiny smoke rings would float out and up into the air.

As a kid, I had lice a time or two...or three. I caught them again while living with Billy Jack. Mom treated my hair with medicine to kill all the bugs but didn't pick out the nits. Instead, she sent me into a salon for a haircut. Mom gave me the money, as well as a tip, to pay the lady for when it was my turn. I waited alone in the clip joint; Mom waited outside in the van toking it up with Billy Jack. The stylist had barely started on my hair when she noticed the nits. She explained that she couldn't cut my hair because I had head lice, then directed me outside to Mom. By the time I made it to the van, I was completely mortified and crying. Mom got defensive and said, "They're all dead, though." She just never seemed to have the *oomph* to follow through with things.

On the first of the month, when welfare checks were delivered, Mom and Billy Jack would pay their pot connection a visit to cop weed and make good on any fronts they had received the prior month. While Billy Jack was inside, Mom and I would have alone time in the car. I'd sing her songs like "Bridge Over Troubled Water," which I think I learned in school, and "Amazing Grace," her all-time favorite. She'd always say I was a great singer. Billy Jack always walked out of the house carrying a brown paper bag.

A couple named Don and Tracy moved into the duplex across the street from us and became Mom and Billy Jack's new pot connection. They had moved to California from Tampa, Florida. For whatever reason, soon after that my family packed up and moved to Dover, Oklahoma. In Dover, it was interesting to see so many brick houses—and grocery bags with written instructions for what to do in case of a tornado. We didn't stay away from California long, just part of a summer, but I remember a day when a cop was following us. Driving through a residential neighborhood, Billy Jack nonchalantly pulled into a stranger's driveway like it was ours. The cop drove on by. After a few minutes, we pulled out and were on our way.

When we made it back to California, we moved in with Billy Jack's mom, Grandma Irma, on the outskirts of Stockton. Her house was older, sizeable, and the interior walls were covered in pictures, mostly black and white, of her family. I had my own room again, this time with another bunk bed set. At bedtime, I'd pop one of Grandma Irma's eight-tracks into the stereo that sat atop my dresser. My favorite was Lobo and the song "You and Me and a Dog Named Boo." After sharing with Mom that I wanted to rescue all the stray animals in the world when I grew up, I'd fall asleep dreaming of a big house on a large piece of property filled with them. Mom always laughed in agreement with whatever plans I made.

At Grandma Irma's, I played in the front yard and on the street. Billy Jack had gotten rid of all his hounds except one, and now raised fighting cocks. The backyard was full of pens of them, plus one with doves that I cared for.

In fifth grade, I left August and went to a school that I eventually loved, Waverly. Most of the students there seemed to come from affluent families, which was different from my previous school. I was unable to fit in at first, my family being so poor and unusual, but a girl named Angel befriended me. One day, she and her sidekick, Melanie, were goofing off in the street in front of our house. When Melanie accidentally tripped Angel and made her fall, Angel screamed "You fucking pussy!" at the top of her lungs. Billy Jack heard it from inside the house and exploded out the front door telling Angel to go home and me that I couldn't hang out with them anymore.

Eventually I became friends with Julie, Wendy, and Helen—a group of girls who were all straight-A students, and nothing like Angel. The worst you might hear out of their mouths was "hell" or "damn." They were polite, and like me, even nice to Chrissy, a student at Waverly who had cerebral palsy, when many others weren't. I heeded my mom's warning: "Don't make fun of people with disabilities, because it might happen to you."

In fifth grade, I decided I wanted to go in a different direction than the rest of my family and made my first stand. One evening, as everyone sat smoking pot in the living room of Grandma Irma's house, when they passed the joint to me, I simply said, "No, I don't want to smoke it anymore." Everyone regarded me in the most peculiar way.

Looking perplexed herself, as she exhaled her hit, Mom casually said, "It's okay. You don't have to smoke if you don't want to."

After that, everybody passed it around or over me. Sometimes they'd forget and pass it to me, and I'd just pass it along to the next person. If anyone said anything about it, Mom would support me by saying, "Jenny wants a different life; she wants to live, not just exist."

Grandma Irma was a Christian woman who regularly attended church, but that didn't diminish her sense of humor. Over her bathroom toilet, a sign read: "Stand close, it's shorter than you think." Grandma Irma was bold. She wasn't afraid to tell me when it was time to start wearing a bra, or how to sit properly in her chair. Even though it was a two-dollar find at a yard sale, she explained that it wasn't the cost of something that was important, but, rather, how it was taken care of. Grandma Irma might have been nosy, too. She pissed Mom off when she found letters from "Jenny's dad" under Mom and Billy Jack's bed. That's how I learned Mom had held on to some sentimental items from one of my fathers: letters from a jail stay. I still don't know which dad.

From Grandma Irma's, we moved back to town into a tiny duplex next door to Lori and Stacy's—they'd become and remained a couple—which was just down the street from Mom and Billy Jack's pot connection—Don and Tracy—who'd recently moved, too. Mom and Billy Jack slept on the living room floor. I shared a bedroom with Ronny, Billy Jack's oldest son, who came to live with us. Ronny wanted to be president one day, and to paint our room red, white, and blue. In lieu of paint, he had an

American flag on his side; I had a "Don't Tread on Me" on mine. Teresa had separated from Rick, so she and their daughter, Amber, had the second bedroom for a short while. Teresa, who was nineteen years old at the time, refused to respect Billy Jack's curfew and would sneak in and out of our home at night. Billy Jack disciplined her in his own way: a smack to the head with our rotary telephone. Mom, taking Billy Jack's side, screamed at Teresa: "You guys always ruin it for me!"

Our duplex was directly behind a crazy lady's house. A tall chain-link fence separated us. She'd stand on her side and cuss for no reason. I knew most of the bad words, but there were a few new ones I'd ask Mom about.

"Mom, is cocksucker a bad word?"

She'd laugh. "Yes."

On a rare visit, Grandma Maggie got out of her blue Chevy Nova and started walking toward our front door. The crazy lady got out of her yard somehow and approached Grandma, then slapped the glasses off her face. Distraught, Grandma got right back into her car and left. That was the closest she ever made it into any of our houses. I imagine if she had that day, it would have been another slap in the face given our home was a far cry from the one she'd raised Mom in.

Don and Tracy brought Tracy's mom and her sister—Anne—from Florida to live with them. Anne, a tall, fair-skinned blonde with a Floridian accent, was my age and became my best friend. She wasn't allowed to stay overnight anywhere, so I found the courage to stay (my first overnight away from home ever) at her place. Don and Tracy eventually bought a much larger two-story house with a duplex on the lot that Anne and her mom lived in, which was a good move for Anne's sake.

Don made a living by craw-dadding. He would catch crayfish in wire cages, sort and rinse them on large screened tables in his backyard, and sell them. He also dealt in pounds of pot. I once watched him carry a big black garbage bag full of it through his house. With a joint hanging from his lip and a hop in his step, Don walked around wearing old-style gym shorts that were too short. It was obvious that he didn't wear underwear, because as his short, dark, curly hair bobbed up and down in synch with his steps, his "American eagle," as Billy Jack called it, would sometimes fall out. When it happened, Mom would give a look of utter disgust, but even that never curtailed the families' get-togethers.

Don fed, clothed, and housed both Anne and her mother; therefore, they were under his rule. He was loud, bossy, and always riding somebody's case—except when he was smiling through the window at Anne and me taking a bath together. Another pervert! Anne told her mother, who was afraid to tell Tracy for fear of them being kicked out.

Anne had a lot of chores around Don and Tracy's house: babysitting, laundry, and always the dishes. I had never been charged with chore duty, ever, so I enjoyed helping. It so happened that eventually my clothes were neatly folded in my own dresser drawers, as Anne had finally convinced me that you really can fit more clothes into a drawer if they are folded, not stuffed. Preparing dinner one evening, Anne, her mom, and I were peeling potatoes. Don came in complaining that we were cutting too much flesh away with the peel. I was afraid of him and didn't want to do anything wrong. I peeled my next potato carefully and slowly. When I was finished, Anne and her mother looked at each other, then smiled at me. I hadn't noticed, but my potato looked like I had carved a man's private parts out of it. I turned red, we all laughed, and then I tossed it into the pot of boiling water—our tribute to the commanding officer.

Since we lived in town again, I went back to August School, but just for the first part of the sixth grade. Anne and I were in the same class. Friends first, competitive second, we'd sit at the front of the room and strive to do our best. We attended a district spelling bee at the local mall together. Anne was out right away by misspelling the word "bathe" and I made it to fourth place before misspelling the word "repetition." There were no hard feelings between us. After school, we would hang out together listening to Hall and Oates records. I can still hear Anne singing "Maneater."

After our duplex, we rented an old white house that was right around the corner from Grandma Irma's. It sat way back in its lot and had a huge front yard which was soon filled with little teepees with fighting cocks tethered to them. Ronny lived with us permanently now, and his oldest sister, her boyfriend, and their young son were staying with us as well. My mother took in Billy Jack's kids just as Billy Jack had taken in me and my siblings. We became a family; an odd family, but a family.

I started back at Waverly in the middle of the sixth grade, and regrouped with Julie, Wendy, and Helen, the straight-A students. I was still focused on a different life, and still loved school and learning. I was comfortable at Waverly and better able to fit in—as long as my friends didn't want to come to my house.

When the day for my sixth-grade science camp trip arrived, I was nervous because, except for Anne's house, I'd never spent a night away from home. Science camp meant I would be away a full seven days. That morning, in our beat-up Ford Maverick, Mom and Billy Jack pulled into the school's bus zone to drop me off. The rear window of our car had been broken out, and the metal edges were sharp and rusty. Luckily the tailpipe smoked heavily, because it covered up the marijuana scent wafting from the car when Mom opened the door. As I stepped out, all the other sixth graders were standing there with their luggage and sleeping bags waiting for the bus to arrive. James, Julie's boyfriend, snarked, "Nice car, Jennifer." It seemed like the bus was never going to get there, but once I was seated it was all good.

Science camp was a blast. Our group explored the grounds of the Del Monte Forest. I kissed a banana slug. We sang campfire songs. And, during a square dance, at a time when Michael Jackson was "in," a camp counselor look-alike picked me out of everybody to dance with him. All the girls were crazy about the guy and, at that moment, envious of me. Part of our seven-day trip was a visit to Pebble Beach. There, Julie, James, Helen, and Wendy buried me in smooth, colorful pebbles. We were told not to take any of the stones from the area, but, *unfortunately,* some got stuck in the cuffs of my rolled-up pant legs. At the end of each day, I slept soundly in the top bunk of our cabin called "Sandy II."

I continued at Waverly for the seventh grade. That year, we did a lot of writing. I wrote a short story about a god named

Crocus that lived on the clouds. When Crocus was happy, the day would be sunny, as the clouds would be high in the sky. When he was sad, it would be dark, as the clouds would be heavy and low. His tears were rain. To my surprise, I won Writer of the Month.

Through all my family's moves, Waverly was my favorite school. I typically made honor roll, but during the seventh grade I pulled all A's except for one B, the price I paid for not being able to do oral book reports. When those were due, I'd sit nervously with clammy hands as my turn approached. Luckily, my friends always had my back. One of them would ask the student assigned to call out turns that day to skip over my name, and he or she would. When the teacher asked if I had given my presentation, because he couldn't recall it, I'd lie and say, "Yes. Yes, I did it already."

It was as if I led a double life. At Waverly I enjoyed learning and achieving good grades; at home I enjoyed helping Billy Jack weigh and bag marijuana to sell—but I didn't smoke it. I received accolades from him for both: "Right on!" My biggest worry was my two lives colliding. Mom often criticized, "Jenny, you're going to have stomach ulcers before you make it to an adult because you fret about everything all the time." Marijuana was everywhere in our house, roaches and half-burned joints in the ashtrays, what was there to worry about? My worst fear was our home being raided and on the front page of the newspaper for all my school friends and their parents to see, or—a close second—my school friends dropping in unannounced and seeing our lifestyle and dump of a home. While I was spared a surprise visit from my friends because their parents forbid them—*whew!*—I didn't escape the raid.

Billy Jack had a marijuana plant that became a tree growing along the back fence of our lot. Eventually, it reached the top of the fence, then higher. Billy Jack, Mom, and I were pulled over while driving in town one afternoon. Cops frisked Billy Jack at the side of our car as other cops went to search our house. We arrived home to find the officers, looking for contraband, had ransacked the place. Everything we owned was strewn about. Even my belongings had been gone through. A homemade cubby that I'd made from a graham cracker box wrapped in aluminum foil was ripped down off my wall, emptied, and tossed onto the floor. The police found the "tree," some pot, and someone's rig, but missed a crockpot full of marijuana in the kitchen above the refrigerator. I have no idea if it made the paper for all my friends and their parents to see, but the next day at school, I felt like it was front-page news.

Neither Billy Jack nor Mom did any time in jail over the raid that I knew of, but shortly after, they decided we'd move north, to Oroville, in Butte County. Most of Billy Jack's relatives had already relocated there, including all his nieces and nephews. Lori and Stacy had, too. I remember the day Lori told Mom and Billy Jack about how great Oroville was. She said, enthusiastically, "It's like almost every other house there has meth!" So, that was the plan. Teresa stayed in Stockton, but the rest of us packed up to move to Oroville.

CHAPTER FIVE

IF YOU'RE SO SMART, WHY AREN'T YOU RICH?

We'd live happily ever after in our cozy little place on the periphery of my family...

Billy Jack's brother, Uncle Henry—who had come down from Oroville to assist with our move north—brought along a helper. When I stepped inside our house, he was standing where the kitchen met the living room. Slightly older than me, he wore a black T-shirt, 501s, and white tennis shoes. He had brown hair, blue eyes, and facial hair (already) that was neatly shaven into a goatee around his uplifting smile. His eyebrows raised when we made eye contact. I was startled that this person was seeing our disaster of a home, even on a good day, including my very own bedroom. He turned to pick up a box, and I read the words on his backward baseball cap: "If you're so smart, why aren't you rich?" I was later told his name was Jonny Jackson, and he was a family friend. After everything was loaded into the trucks, we followed Uncle Henry—and Jonny—north.

We made it to Oroville in two hours. I remember driving on the main road, Oroville Dam Boulevard, and seeing the mountains in the background surrounding the valley. When we reached the middle of town, we pulled into our new driveway across the street from Las Plumas High School, which I later learned Jonny, a sophomore, attended. From the outside, the medium-sized house looked nice and clean, which was typically how we started our rentals. The yard was spacious and fenced—and soon covered with chicken pens and rooster teepees.

Once we were moved in, Mom enrolled me in Palermo School. To get there, I had to walk to Helen Wilcox Elementary and catch a bus that hauled me across town. Palermo School was nothing like Waverly. It was much larger and very dark. On my first day, in homeroom, the teacher called me up to the front of the class. I walked up the center aisle between all the students. After he checked my name off the roster, he asked, "Where are you from?"

"Stockton," I replied.

Then he asked, in front of everybody, "Why'd you come up here?" He sounded disappointed.

Too embarrassed to say anything, as I sank in my shoes, I just shrugged my shoulders.

Whether I was walking to and from the bus stop, sitting in class, or outside during recess, I kept to myself as much as possible at Palermo. I did my best to not be noticed, hoping if I didn't see any of the other kids, they wouldn't see me. Jonny rolled up our driveway on his bicycle one day laughing: "I saw you walking to the bus stop this morning. I was calling your name. You didn't hear me?" I had no idea what he was talking about, but wished I had.

Jonny lived in Southside, the bad part of Oroville. His mom and dad were still married, something I didn't see very often. Always willing to help people, like he did with our move, Jonny would hop on his bicycle and answer calls with the fire department. A clean-cut guy, when others his age were wearing parachute pants and playing hacky sack, he never strayed from his simple 501s. He didn't use tobacco either, so he didn't reek of smoke or have yellow teeth.

Jonny and my family spent Easter that year thirty miles north of Oroville in small mountainy Concow, where Uncle Henry lived. At Crain Park, we barbecued and played baseball. We took turns riding bikes through a culvert under the road that dumped us into a large ditch full of water. Uncoordinated, I lost control of my bike every time and nearly drowned, but it was fun. I could get past the embarrassment of what I must have looked like doing it, too, even when it was Jonny who was laughing at me. He was quite skilled on his bicycle.

From where I stood, the only thing good about our move to Oroville was Jonny. After school, he'd find reasons to stop by our house. Once he dropped in to ask my parents if they were interested in buying a set of encyclopedias for his school's fundraiser. Billy Jack got mad and told him, "Don't bother coming around if you're going to try and sell us anything." Apparently, Billy Jack still disliked solicitors.

Another time, given Billy Jack's love for fowl, Jonny brought over a (dead) chicken to impress him. I'm not sure whether it was a rooster or a hen, but while riding to our house after dark, he noticed it on a fence. "I think it had a heart attack, because it just keeled over when I grabbed it!" he exclaimed. I can still hear the embarrassment in Jonny's laughter. My stepdad wasn't the slightest bit moved.

Billy Jack was nothing short of a jackass to Jonny, but Mom was always kind to him. If he was at our house at dinnertime, she was happy to serve him a plate of food. More accurately, she'd make his plate and then have me serve him. After eating, Jonny and I would horse around, often by sailing matchbooks and bottlecaps across the room at each other with the snap of our fingers—being especially successful with a good tag when the other wasn't looking. He spent part of his sixteenth birthday with us, showing off his new white Pumas and eyeglasses that his mother had bought him. His lenses changed tint depending on the lighting. His puzzled chuckle when he talked about his mother that evening still echoes in my mind: "My mom spelled my middle name with two N's, D-A-N-N-I-E-L. Is it Daniel? Danielle? What was she thinking?"

Two and a half years older, Jonny seemed interested in me, and I was interested in him. He began calling my mom "Mom" and me "Jennie-fer." When I met his father, his dad commented, "Jon, you're moving up in the world." We weren't allowed to officially "go out" until October, when I turned fourteen, but everything felt perfect. With REO Speedwagon's recently released "Can't Fight This Feeling" playing in my head, I'd drift off to sleep every night dreaming about our future together: we'd get married—unlike my mom, I'd be married only once—we'd get jobs, a car, and an apartment. When we had children, our daughter would be named Jonni Dannielle, middle named spelled with two N's, just like her dad. We'd live happily ever after in our cozy little place on the periphery of my family.

I can't remember whether Jonny smoked pot along my family right away or not, but he eventually did. I still chose not to. But one day, as if some sort of soothsayer, Ronny, who also smoked, told Mom and me about a dream he had. He said that I decided to stop being a "good girl" and started to drink, smoke, and get into trouble. I thought that was absurd. With a disturbed look on her face, Mom snarked, "Well, I hope that doesn't come true."

Concow, where Uncle Henry lived, had been named after the Native American Concow Maidu tribe—and was best known for its marijuana gardens. As my (bad) luck would have it, the isolated mountain community comprised merely of the Dome Store, a post office, gas station, hardware shop, park, and two restaurants with bars appealed to my parents. I didn't want to leave Oroville—especially Jonny—but that summer we moved to the sticks to live in a single-wide trailer surrounded by nothing but red dirt that, as usual, was soon covered with cages and teepees for Billy Jack's fighting chickens.

Living in Concow meant that to see Jonny I had to rely on chance encounters whenever my parents went into town, which was typically only around the first and fifteenth of the month, because that was when welfare checks came in and they had money for gasoline and supplies. When Jonny and I did meet up, he'd sometimes have a present for me. During one run-in, sitting on his bicycle in my cousin Chad's driveway, he handed me a small, red, heart-shaped pillow. Another time, I received a rectangular green one with the word "love" ironed onto it.

―――――

Mom made sure I had new clothes at the beginning of every school year, but when eighth grade began, I started out with five outfits, and each had its own pair of matching shoes. That was more than I had ever gotten at one time. Most students at Concow School lived in poverty. When I wore a different getup each day of the week, some of the kids looked at me like I was from a well-off family. That was a first. At Waverly, it had been the opposite. Head lice don't discriminate, however. Early in September, I started to feel the familiar itch. Infestation was confirmed when a louse jumped from my head onto the page of my math book. Teachers pulled all of us in one by one to check our hair, and then sent the pest-ridden students home. Thankfully, that was the last time I ever caught it.

Trying to settle into my new school, I carefully sought out the good students for friends and avoided the troubled ones. I tried to slide under the radar by not getting too close or personal with anyone. To begin with, I befriended Eva, a straight-A student. The first time I visited her house, her parents asked me what mine did for a living. "My stepdad is in construction," I fibbed. I didn't want to get caught lying, so I distanced myself from her. I'd sit alone on the bench at recesses, until I later hooked up with Brooke.

Brooke was the most disliked and, at times, belligerent girl in our school. She was a year younger than I was, but smoked cigarettes already. Always upset at someone, she wore a lot of large rings on her fingers just in case she had to fight. Sometimes she would get in trouble for talking back to the teachers, or even punching the school lockers. I felt it best to be on her good side. We became acquaintances first, then close friends. Once referred to as her "sidekick," I and my submissiveness offset her defiance, and we managed to keep each other out of trouble.

With Brooke by my side and Jonny in my future, I felt tough—not mean, but brave and strong. I still feared the beastly oral reports, but, gaining confidence, I pushed myself to do a presentation in front of the class. It was about Dentyne gum. "Dentyne cleans your teeth when you chew, so choose Dentyne," the last line of my report read. On my way back to my seat, a kid named Jacob laughed and said it was stupid. I already knew that. I was just proud to have survived it.

Playing the alto saxophone sounded much cooler than the clarinet, so I switched it up. (The school owned the sax, so Mom couldn't hock it.)

Furthering my bravery, I tried out for cheerleading with Brooke. The judges could hardly hear my soft voice, but because it was a small school and anyone who tried out made it, we both ended up on the team.

I could have sat it out, but in performing arts class I recited "Little Boy Blue" on stage. To my embarrassment, everyone in the audience laughed when I got it backward and said, "The cow's in the meadow and the sheep's in the corn." I made a comeback, though, by rattling my chains as Marley's ghost in *A*

Christmas Carol and strumming an air guitar to Def Leppard's "Too Late for Love" in the talent show.

My family's landlord, Pearl, a tiny elderly widow, gave me a job. On weekends, I cleaned her rentals when tenants moved out, mowed her lawn and fruit orchard, stacked firewood, and harvested and planted flower bulbs in her garden. At lunchtime, she'd serve me my favorite sandwich, a Reuben, without the sauerkraut (if that's still considered a Reuben). At $3.50 an hour, I earned enough money to buy myself things that I needed, like new clothes, as well as some things that I wanted, like cigarettes when I took up smoking. My mom's only reaction when that happened was, without faltering, to bum a couple off me.

The thirty-mile drive and two-and-a-half-year age gap between Jonny and me had grown to more like 300 miles and a decade. A junior in high school now, he must not have been in as much of a hurry to "go out" as I was, because my fourteenth birthday came and went. It didn't help me that Dana, my mother-of-two "cougar" cousin, had gotten ahold of him. I distinctly remember the look of disgust on Mom's face when Dana sheepishly divulged that it was Jonny who had left the monkey bites on her neck.

February rolled around, February 4 to be exact, and Jonny finally asked me, by way of a telephone call, to be his girlfriend. Of course, I said yes. On Valentine's Day, I arranged to meet him at Lori and Stacy's—they now had two small children—where he hung out when he wasn't in school. With money that I had earned, I bought him a giant Hershey's Kiss. In return, I got a heart-shaped box of chocolates. The gap between us disappeared.

Once Jonny had his driver's license, he'd borrow his mom's Dodge Aries and drive up to Concow to see me. Later he came in his Ford Ranger pickup. Visiting me in Concow one night, Jonny and I crashed on my living room floor. I managed to maneuver so I could hold his hand underneath his pillow. He called me on it the next morning with his silly smile and "You're funny, Jennie-fer" look. It was all good.

Clowning around one afternoon, from the cover of my bedroom door, with a Polaroid camera in hand, I ambushed him sitting on the worn-out recliner in our living room and captured his perfect smile. Between the time I snapped the photo and the film fully developed, I don't think he took his eyes off me once.

When Jonny got his motorcycle, the "rice burner," as he'd call it, even though he wore riding glasses behind his bike's windshield, he always arrived at my house with a bug in one of his eyes. I was happy to carefully dig it out. One afternoon, he picked me up from a basketball game that I'd cheered at. Wearing my green and gold uniform, I had him first take me home to change. Then, snugly seated, we went for a picturesque ride up to the Oroville Dam.

On weekends, I stayed at my cousin Chad's house to meet up with Jonny. One night, after he picked me up from Concow on his motorcycle, we arrived at Chad's before anyone else. Unable to enter the house, Jonny pulled a sleeping bag from his cargo carrier and rolled it out onto the front lawn. There was room enough for two inside, but he respectfully zipped me up in it solo. We hung out talking under the night sky until Chad and his wife, Katie, arrived and let us in.

At Chad's, I often cuddled with Jonny on the couch, wallowing in the scent of his musk cologne. I enjoyed playing with his chest hair, especially through a tiny hole in his shirt if I could find one. When he couldn't take it anymore, I'd get a chuckle and an "Ow! What are you doing? Stop it, Jennie-fer." Then we'd reconfigure our bodies. With his arms holding me, I'd wrap mine around him, place my leg over and between his, and bury my face in his shoulder. That was my favorite place. We'd lie that way until his mom came knocking on the door to tell him it was time to go home.

I was far from happy about living in the boonies, but mountainy Concow did have another side, and it was quite refreshing. Off Jordan Hill Road was the best swimming spot. Clear, cold water ran among huge boulders. It was the first in a series of twelve or better teacup holes you'd find if you braved the uphill hike. The third was for skinny-dipping (I went there once, but it was much later). With warm weather upon us, Jonny accompanied my mom and me to the *other* side of Concow. Mom sat on a blanket on the bank, wearing cutoffs and a tank top that covered her halter-top bathing suit, her auburn-dyed hair in a ponytail. With her eyes hidden behind large sunglasses, she spent the afternoon happily rolling and toking joints. I lay content on a rock, soaking up the sun in my leopard print bikini (Brooke and I had bought matching suits); Jonny stood waist high in the water, brushing his pecs, surprised at how cold that water *really* was.

When Jonny and I couldn't be together either in Concow or town, we'd talk on the phone about anything and everything. At the end of each conversation, he'd tell me, "Jennie-fer, I love you. Yep. More than you'll ever know." I believed him.

———

Near the end of the school year, out of nowhere, Mom received a check in the mail. It was the first child support payment ever from my father. The paper said he had been ordered to pay a hundred dollars a month, but welfare took half. Mom gave me the entire fifty dollars to spend. I bought cute, summery matching top-and-shorts outfits. Another check came the following month. The support payments piqued my curiosity about my father, but I had no idea how to approach my mom about it. I knew questions about him would crush her. When I finally found the nerve, I was the one who was crushed, however. Mom had lied—to me—about who my real father was. It wasn't Willy, it was some man named Ivan. She did drugs while pregnant—with me. Born out of wedlock, I was a mistake by my grandfather's, and apparently God's, standards. Even my biological father wanted nothing to do with me. As hard as it was to accept, simply put, I believed I was unlovable, and everyone would have been better off had I not been conceived. I was grateful for Jonny, who loved me, but after spending two days holed up in my room, I stepped out pissed-off and hell-bent on getting back at my mother.

To get even with Mom, the next school day I told Brooke, "I want to get stoned."

She looked at me funny and said, "Really?"

"Yes. It's been a long time."

Next, Brooke and I got caught passing a note in science class asking where to get acid. (I guess I was still curious about what it looked like.) Pulled into the office by the principal, I gave him and my parents a bogus story that the note was referring to battery acid that had eaten a hole through my jeans, which really happened. Nobody bought my lie. Luckily, I only got a warning from the principal and my parents.

Then, walking home from school, I stopped at a classmate's house on Buzzard's Roost Road. He poured me a half a glass of brandy, followed by a half a glass of wine, then I hit the road home. Once there, stumbling into the house, Mom put my drunken butt into a cold tub of water to sober me up.

Mom tried to make peace with me for all her years of lying about who my real father was—like suddenly getting up to make my breakfast before school—but I wanted no part of her. She must have even spoken to Jonny about it because he called: "Mom says you're doing some really bad things. Are you mad?"

"No."

It was *finally* the end of the school year. For graduation, Mom bought me a pale pink and white satin dress with ruffles and lace. It cost seventy dollars, which was a lot of money for us. At the commencement ceremony, with Jonny and my family in the audience, I pushed through my fear of public speaking and gave the introduction. It was short, but I did it. After a slideshow of childhood pictures of the Class of 1986 to the song "Memories," we received our diplomas through "Pomp and Circumstance." Jonny joined me for the dance afterward, although we didn't make it out onto the floor. Neither of us was into fast-dancing, and when Madonna's slow "Crazy for You" came on, apparently his attention was elsewhere. Rather than invite me out into the middle of everyone, he handed my stepbrother Ronny the class paddle to slap the gorgeous Double-D (cup) Hannah Anderson on the ass with. That was awkward. Overall, I still considered it a good night.

High school—and freedom—was on the horizon, and my future with Jonny looked bright. I was confident our life together was going to be great when we were old enough to reach the periphery of my family. Only there was no such thing as "the periphery of my family." That summer, Jonny started spending a lot of time at Lori and Stacy's—who were now manufacturing meth! One afternoon, Mom had to go there to get "something" from Jonny. Of course, I rode along with her. When we pulled into the driveway, Mom told me to wait in the car. Reluctantly, I obeyed. Jonny didn't even bother to come out and talk to me. When Mom returned, she was wired tight. It didn't take much to figure out what she had gotten from my boyfriend! Sensing how angry I was, as we pulled onto the road, a joint between her fingers, she said, "Jenny, marijuana is the only thing I do. I'm sorry if you don't like it." *Such a liar.*

Jonny and I continued to meet up at Chad's, but at times he seemed on edge. I didn't understand why. Chad's wife, Katie, noticed it, too, and thought maybe he was getting impatient with how our relationship wasn't moving forward physically—we'd been together six months and hadn't even shared a real kiss yet. As he said goodnight to me one evening, Katie told him, "Hey, give her a real kiss!"

Sounding irritated, he came back with, "She doesn't give me any signs that she wants me to!"

She told me, "Just attack him!"

Well, that would never happen, but he finally did make a move and we shared a real kiss.

After that night, the kisses were long. Standing next to his motorcycle in my driveway, we'd end our visits with a lengthy one. Billy Jack would get mad; Mom would tell him not to worry about it.

The kisses were long, but infrequent. Our phone contact and get-togethers at Chad's place became rare. One time when Jonny made it there, as if transformed into a different person, he was frustrated that someone didn't give him what they "owed" him. The kid who once hopped on his bicycle and responded to calls with the fire department was now complaining about what he was "owed." My heart sank a little more the day I overheard Stacy bragging that he'd offered Jonny a line of meth in exchange for worming Lori's and his dog. My worst fear, that Jonny was doing meth, was confirmed later when I overheard Lori say, "But he only drinks it, in coffee or tea."

I wasn't sure if Jonny was distancing himself from me because he wanted out of our relationship—like every other male in my life had—or because of meth, the "fuck" drug. It never crossed my mind to wait until I was eighteen for anything. In a telephone conversation, I told him, "I'll be out on my own by the time I'm seventeen."

He laughed at me like I was being silly, then asked, "And how are you going to do that?"

"I don't know. I'll get a job."

Waiting alone one night for Jonny at Chad's, I memorized all but the very last sentence of the poem that was tacked on the wall above the couch where we spent so much time together.

Ode to a Fallen Star

If in the course of a man's lifetime, he is fortunate enough to find one true love; one soul who would exist for his own sake alone; one star who would shine and light the path that they as one would travel, then, as a man, he would dare to live as no mortal would dare. He would love beyond all possible limits with only one thought in his mind, and that thought would be that star. To exist for someone special and know that she in return exists for you, Love becomes the binder if it is deep and true. But when his world has crumbled to dust and to dirt, and all that he has left is deep pain and unending hurt, he realizes that today greets him with nothing to find, for his love has flown and there is no time. There exists in that once filled cavern of his mind the thoughts of yesterday's wonderful times. But today and tomorrow escape in the steam, of that erupting volcano of dead buried dreams. He never forgets the past and its mar, for he always remembers that once bright fallen star. And after much struggle, he reaches to find another bright star with a much brighter shine.

T.H.E. Moon[1]

Little did I know, had I changed the male pronouns to female, the poem would soon prove to be all too fitting.

Back at home, Mom warned me about staying at Chad's

---

1 Over the years, I've looked for the author of this poem, but the original source remains a mystery.

house. She said, "I don't want what happened to me to happen to you." I knew what had happened to her but had no idea why there was suddenly concern for my safety at Chad's. Soon after Mom's warning, hoping that Jonny might drop by, I stayed there anyway. As I lay half asleep in the living room of the quiet house, several people were milling about. One cousin was searching the backyard, one was searching the attic, and one walked stealthily behind the couch I was resting on. I sat up slowly and looked at him. He was carrying a rifle.

He said, "*Hush*. Someone's at the door." He watched the knob. "See that?"

Not knowing what this person was doing, or if someone was really at the door, I lay frozen in fear.

He took a kitchen chair into the bathroom, then stepped up onto it and looked through the access hole into the attic. He whispered up there, "They're in the attic." When he stepped down, he walked to the kitchen door. I heard him check the lock. He then walked behind the sofa to the front door. He turned the knob, opened the door, and went outside. He fired the gun, came back in, and closed the door. "That car that just went by was a cop; the dog chased after him," he told me. I just lay there, afraid to move or say anything. The cousin walked around to the front of the couch. With the rifle in his hand, he knelt and placed the gun parallel to me, on the cushion. He slipped his hand under my blanket and whispered, *"Hush."* After a short time, he left the living room. He later came back and knelt beside me again, but this time without the rifle.

I politely said, "No."

He said, "Okay," stood up, and left.

I never stayed there again.

I spent a split-second wondering if Jonny would want anything to do with me if he ever found out what happened; I spent many more certain he wouldn't.

CHAPTER SIX

THE "WHY" IN THE ROAD

Mom would write the list of bills every month...

We had lived in Concow for just over a year, and our home screamed poverty. Our single-wide trailer with two small bedrooms plus a large one added on housed Billy Jack, Mom, Ronny, and me, then Billy Jack's other son Lonny and daughter Marcy as well. Eventually, Lori and Stacy's now three young children—Samantha (Sam), Stephanie, and Steven— moved in. At any given time, there were between four and nine people living in our trailer.

Mom would write the list of bills every month. At the top she put Billy Jack's and her pot connection, next was rent, then utilities, and food was always last. I never saw her exchange Food Stamps at a two-for-one ratio, a hundred dollars in stamps for fifty dollars in cash, like many people did, but by the end of every month we were down to powdered milk with flour-and-water pancakes, or "Indian Bread," topped with sugar-water syrup. If you added a little vanilla and sugar—when we had it—the powdered milk wasn't supposed to taste so bad.

Mom cleaned, but there was only so much she could do. The trailer was set in nothing but red dirt that got tracked in all the time and ended up everywhere. And with little to no money, she didn't have the tools she needed to do a thorough job. In our small kitchen, the stove had gunk caked under the burners. The walls and backsplash were covered in greasy amber specks that wouldn't budge no matter how hard you scrubbed. I know, because I tried. When cabinet handles or knobs fell off, I was the one who cared enough to put them back on. We had cockroaches here, too, especially noticeable in the kitchen at night when you surprised them with the light. They loved our microwave. When I'd catch them in there, since I was told they could live through a nuclear war, I'd turn it on high. When they started to scurry, however, I'd turn it off. I didn't have the heart to put even a nasty cockroach to the test.

Mom would sweep the kitchen linoleum floor with her broom that was missing half its bristles, then pick up the dirt pile with her "an old Indian trick" of wetting the edge of a sheet of newspaper, sticking it to the floor, and then sweeping it onto it. That worked well, because you could wipe up any residual dust lines with the wet part. That wasn't the only way newspaper was recycled at our house—it was particularly useful in the bathroom at the end of every month when we went without the necessities that normal people had. Newspaper gets surprisingly soft if you crumple it long enough.

In the living room, whenever Mom swept the carpet, the top layer of dirt rose and sent particles everywhere. When she dusted, she'd straighten the old newspapers, magazines—typically the *National Enquirer, Gamecock,* and *TV Guide*—and junk mail that was scattered among the rolling papers, lighters, and ashtrays full of cigarette butts and marijuana roaches.

Our bathroom was small and cluttered. The toilet was unspeakable. Aside from the seat and an occasional swirl of the bowl with a brush, I don't know if it had ever really been cleaned. It was as if the stain had eaten into the porcelain.

The thought of being a freshman in high school scared me, but visiting town—escaping the sticks—five days a week sounded appealing. When it came time to enroll, to start off on a good foot, I included college prep courses in my schedule. In band, I'd continue to play the sax. I chose French for my foreign language. I don't really know why I picked French—maybe it sounded romantic, or maybe because I was born at the San Joaquin County General Hospital in French Camp, California. Oroville High, where I'd be going, and Las Plumas High, where Jonny went, were across town from one other, but Jonny had his motorcycle, so I had high hopes of us doing the things young couples were supposed to do—like spending time together and going off campus for lunch. I almost couldn't wait for that first day to arrive.

Once school started, it was difficult; not academically, but because I didn't fit in, except with Brooke. Trying to find our place outside of class, she and I mingled with the preppies once, but that was quite awkward. More appropriately, we settled in with the stoners. Brooke didn't like a girl named Amy in that

group. Fighting still made me afraid, even if I wasn't a participant, so on the day that Brooke planned to "kick her ass," I
stayed home "sick." What a friend I was. When Brooke wasn't at
school, I hung out solo. Luckily, I was alone when I went into the
girls' bathroom to remove what I thought was a sticker caught
between my thigh and tapered Levi's, because a cockroach
crawled out instead. I wanted to die. News like that would have
spread like wildfire around campus.

It seemed as if Jonny had forgotten he had a girlfriend; he
made no more effort to see me in town during the school week
than he had over the summer. Surprisingly, he did show up during
lunch recess on my fifteenth birthday. Straddling his motorcycle,
he handed me a bouquet of flowers and gave me a long kiss. For
laughs, I wanted to show him the weathered "Carla Roberts +
Jonny Jackson" I'd found carved into the awning of the picnic
table in the break area, but before I could, he was gone again. I
didn't get it: *Does he love me or not?* I mostly felt like not.

In time, an old Indian drug dealer from Concow everybody
called "Uncle" began showing up after school to "kidnap" the
stoner kids, which came to include Brooke and me, in his green
Chevy Nova. With a bottle of peach schnapps to pass around
and a joint to share, he'd deliver us wherever we wanted on the
mountain. For good grades, he'd hand out green bud, but I never
got any of that because my grades were lousy. He did, however,
give me a bud for when I needed to bribe my mom.

"Mom, can I go to Brooke's?"

"You were there for three days straight."

"I'll bring you a joint."

"Okay."

Since Chad's house was no longer an option, I stayed at Lori and Stacy's sometimes, because that's where I could find Jonny. Even when we were in the same house, he kept his distance. There was no cuddling on the couch or watching TV anymore. I didn't understand why. One night I brought a bottle of Jack Daniels to get his attention. Amused by me, he took a swig, then asked, "What are you doing, Jennie-fer?" I crashed where I made our bed; he crashed on the couch after staying up most of the night cleaning my sister's house.

Another time at Lori and Stacy's, I feared my two-year-old niece had been exposed to meth since there was a lab in the back of the house. She was talking gibberish—like my mom when she was wired—and going room to room, rearranging her toys. When she'd get them perfectly situated, she'd pick them up and move them to the next room, and then start all over again. Everyone in the house was wired and up all night, except me; I fell fast asleep. I awoke in the early morning hours when my niece crawled into my bed.

My relationship with Jonny continued to grow distant, until I got "the call." He said that he was going to Iowa to take care of a sick—female!— friend.

"Iowa?"

Because I had pronounced it "ahy-OH-uh" he chuckled and corrected me: "You say it "AHY-uh-wuh."

No matter how you say it, I took it as his way out of our relationship. Stunned that he would really leave me, all I could say was, "Okay."

Free—and alone—I became interested in a cutie my age from Concow. At a party on New Year's Eve, I gave him my virginity—his only interest. It turned out I wasn't the only girl on the mountain he had done that to.

In February of my freshman year, I became involved with Eric, a young musician whose family had moved to Concow from Los Angeles. Tall, handsome, and nineteen, with blond hair just past his shoulders, he'd practice his acoustic guitar and play a song he wrote about "the girl with the long brown hair"—yours truly! Even though he was of age and I wasn't, I took him home to meet my mom and get permission for him to take me to the school's winter formal dance. Mom said okay. Eric and I, along with Brooke and her date, attended the event together. Dolled up, we spent the evening dancing under a dazzling strobe light to the beat of eighties' music.

Every day after school, Eric picked me up at the bus stop at Concow Road and Highway 70. One afternoon, as I hopped into his beat-up Toyota truck, he began talking about his future. "I think I want to become a counselor," he said. "It would be cool to talk to people all day for fifty bucks an hour." I enjoyed him sharing his vision with me. At his house, holding me as I sat on the edge of his truck's bed, he said, "You know what, Ferp?" (My childhood nickname "Fer" had evolved to "Ferp.")

"What?"

As he lifted me from the side of the truck bed to carry me into the house, he said, "I think I love you."

Jonny, who never made it to Iowa, must have heard that I had a boyfriend. He showed up at school during a lunch break and, as if trying to let the world know that I was his, started to lay a kiss on me. When I pulled back, he figured out that things between us weren't the same.

That evening, Eric asked about Jonny's visit. Someone had told him before I could. I explained to him who Jonny was and what happened. Eric had no qualms about it.

Jonny called me later. He said, "I waited for you for a long time."

I had no response.

Mom once said that if I ever ended it with Jonny he might do something terrible; but once we separated, he brought a new girlfriend up to our house to visit. Mom said she looked like a nice girl.

Billy Jack wasn't happy that I was seeing nineteen-year-old Eric, so he started picking me up at the bus stop after school. There was no way I was going to let Billy Jack tell me what to do. As soon as we got home, I'd thumb a ride to Eric's. That made Billy Jack furious. When Eric heard that I had an angry stepdad, he asked me about that, too. I responded, "Billy Jack's nothing to worry about."

During my defiant attempts to be with Eric, someone new and more appropriate for him came into the picture. Just short of three months into our relationship, while carving a "J" for Jennifer out of a piece of wood, he wondered if he should turn it into a "T" for Tori, the new girl. After careful thought, he opted to sever my hook and go with the T. Eric was honest and up front with me throughout the whole ordeal, but that one still hurt.

My next boyfriend was Marty. He wasn't as easy on the eyes

71

as Jonny and Eric, but he was out of school and had a job. Plus, he had a cute little red convertible that he'd sometimes let me drive. Marty drove me twenty-five miles to the town of Paradise to show me a rental where he was hoping we could eventually move in together. I wasn't sure about that. Marty and I were a couple, but most of my time was spent running amok with Brooke.

Like pretty much everyone in Concow, Brooke and I had our very own "Smoky" marijuana pipes. The story with Smoky is that he was an attorney who got tired of the hustle and bustle that came with the job and gave it up to become a recluse. He lived in cut-offs and only showered once a year, on summer solstice. His hands were rough and dirty like the rest of his body, but he made beautiful soapstone pipes. If you spit on them and then wiped it away, the colors were phenomenal.

It was rare to hear someone speak about coke in Concow, but crank, or meth, was everywhere—especially given my sister was cooking it. And unlike Stacy, Lori didn't make you worm dogs for it; all you had to do was ask. Luckily, I knew right away meth wasn't for me, no matter how angry I was.

While at a party, I finally found out what a hit of acid looked like. The next morning, the adult who oversaw the bash handed out vitamins to those who had fried explaining, "Because it takes a lot out of a body."

Uncle continued to "kidnap" the stoner kids after school. One day he dropped me at home, with a bud for my mom of course. When I walked in, she warned: "Jenny, he's going to fall in love with you."

That sounded ridiculous—and sickening. "Mom, that's gross."

Soon after her warning, Uncle, trying to divide Brooke and me, said that she had stolen some weed from him. That was a lie. The next thing I knew, Uncle was brandishing a .357 Magnum at Marty for allegedly stealing from his pot garden. That same day, Uncle met me walking down the road and handed me a Hallmark card. In it he asked me to be his "lady." *Mom was right.* So gross, I tossed the card back at him through his car's window, then gave him a middle finger as he peeled off.

Years later I heard a rumor that the authorities pulled Uncle up from the bottom of Concow Lake. Weighted down with concrete and chains, he was taken out by another drug dealer.

———————

Brooke and I made it through our freshman year. I was ecstatic that school was out and summer was upon us. We were inseparable. She stayed at my house a couple of times, but I stayed at hers often. Hers didn't have electricity, it ran on propane and kerosene lamps, but mine had cockroaches. The last time she stayed at my house, a thirsty Brooke got up in the middle of the night and walked into the kitchen for a drink of water. When she reached up and opened the cupboard for a glass, a cockroach fell into her shirt. Jumping and screaming, she couldn't get it out. Ronny was right there to tease her until she was full-blown crying. Free from infestation, Brooke's house was much more accommodating than mine. Plus, her mom worked, while mine didn't, giving us more privacy and freedom.

During the day, when Brooke's mom was at work, Brooke

would "borrow" their extra car—until she totaled it on a tree and broke her nose. At night, Brooke and I snuck out and hitch-hiked up and down Concow Road to hang at friends' houses. Sometimes we'd stop at the public pool and hop the fence for a swim. On Brooke's fifteenth birthday that July (I was nine months older), we made our way to the Dome Store. Brooke climbed up to the sign and rearranged the letters on it to read "hapi b'day." Everyone in our small community figured out whose birthday it was, even the owner, who didn't seem to mind his new ad.

If I was thumbing it to Brooke's house, which was at the back end of Concow Road, I knew I had better catch a ride be-fore the base of Washeleski's "Killer" Hill; otherwise, cars wouldn't stop, and I would be out of luck on that long, steep uphill grade. To get home, I'd hitch a ride to the corner of Con-cow and Nelson Bar Roads, then walk the two-mile trek down through the deep hairpin corner and up and out into the open to make it to our trailer. If I was walking alone at night, I'd blast my radio to keep wild animals away and wave my arms overhead ev-ery so often to repel bats.

Among our escapades that summer, Brooke started dating an older guy who had an even older friend. That friend was Rick, a self-proclaimed "surfer-hippie-jock." He had a new pickup, and he loved to blare The Doors, ZZ Top, and Bad Company through its sound system. Six-foot-tall, well-built yet slender, with a Tom Selleck mustache, Rick was a good-looking man...who was al-ways drinking beer. He'd tear the tab off his cans; otherwise, when he took a swig, it would get caught under his deformed nostril. He claimed his nostril had been torn by Kurt Russell's cleat during a high school football game. Dude, Rick's obnoxious Pomeranian, would lap up beer alongside him.

Rick, almost twenty years my senior, constantly hit on me. He'd say, "I'll treat you like a queen" and "I'll put your face on a magazine," but my all-time favorite was, "When I'm ninety, you'll be seventy."

I wasn't interested.

He asked if I had ever eaten a good steak, and I said no, so he said he could take me to a place where I could get a top-grade one.

"No. Thank you, though."

He hooked up with a local gal closer to his age, yet still whispered, "I love you," in my ear even when she was standing right there. When that relationship ended, he told me he was leaving Concow for southern California, where "normal, civilized people lived." He invited me to join him.

It sounded appealing, but, "No, I don't think so."

He said he'd return every year until I turned eighteen and wrote me a poem titled "My Dove." The final verse read: *Now I'll shed a tear, for I'll have to wait another year.*

———

My feelings toward being a sophomore were no different from being a freshman: I hated it. On the first day of school, in every class from English to geography to science, I sat in the very back of the room and watched each student say their name and something about themselves, sometimes prompting a group discussion—that I would never be a part of. A simple "my name's Jennifer Seifert" is all they got out of me. Even then, I replayed in my head how stupid I'd sounded.

I fell behind right away in all my classes because I wasn't doing my homework. Terrified the teacher would call on me with a question I was sure I wouldn't be able to answer, I avoided school whenever possible by cutting with Brooke. That meant I had to forge Mom's signature on absence notes. I knew I would eventually get caught, and that would hurt my mother, but I didn't care. Hurting her had been a long time coming. I hadn't forgotten about her lying to me about my father for all those years—or the day she had to get "something" from my boyfriend at Lori and Stacy's, for that matter. However, just when I thought there was no possible way for her to stoop any lower, she surprised me.

Meth had been present in my home for a year and a half. On this day, a canister of it in liquid form—waste—was tucked away in my closet and a spoon lay atop my dresser. A syringe remained secreted in our bathroom medicine cabinet. None of these items was ever mine. Mom was impatiently pacing around the house. She was waiting for Lori to bring her more meth. Lori was late. In sick desperation, Mom delivered her very own *coup de grace*: "Jenny, do you have any?"

With utter disgust, I answered, "No."

Oddly enough, my Libra horoscope read that I'd be taking an unexpected trip soon. It was September, and I hadn't seen Rick since before school started. He had told Brooke to let me know again that he would be leaving Concow, but he'd be back each year for me.

Brooke and I lay on my bed and discussed whether I should take him up on his offer to go away.

She said, "He loves you."

"Yeah. And he'll never leave me."

I was sure I missed him, but driving Marty's cute little red convertible through the parking lot of the Dome Store, I saw Rick standing there—holding a can of beer. It was as if he had been waiting for me the whole time. Surprised that he hadn't left yet, and since I was a lousy new driver, I landed the car on and over a log that was used as a parking stop. Hindsight is 20-20: Rick wasn't really planning on leaving Concow, at least not then.

A jobless and broke Rick had worn out his welcome with every one of his friends, so he started camping on a hidden trail that was a couple miles from my home. He survived on instant oatmeal, canned goods he'd heat up on his camp stove, and water from the natural spring on Dark Canyon Road. Sometimes I'd bring him food; otherwise, he would consume nothing but beer. He *always* had beer. He'd eat small portions of whatever I brought, because he said his stomach had shrunk from not eating regularly and he didn't want to make the hunger pangs worse when he had to go without food again.

Mom told me that Jonny came by the house to see me on my sweet sixteen. I wasn't home, however; I'd spent it with Rick at a swimming hole. My present from the "surfer-hippie-jock" was a watch that someone had left behind on a rock near the water. Claiming he could get work in the city, he once again brought up the idea of leaving Concow and going where "normal, civilized people lived." He said I could finish high school in one day by taking a GED. Without thinking it through, I chose to forgo the prom, senior cut day, senior pictures, graduation, and every high school reunion to come. Two weeks after I turned sixteen, Rick and I headed down to Sacramento. Four days later, I called my mom to let her know I was okay. She cried, "You're supposed to be with me until you're eighteen." I didn't feel sorry for her.

Much later, Rick confessed that he never intended to have anything more than a fling with me, but from the beginning of our relationship, he wanted us to make a baby. He wanted a girl, and to name her after his mother, Jean. Tiffany Jean would be her name. I went along with anything and everything he wanted.

In Sacramento, Rick hit up his old employers for drywall finishing jobs. One such "bitch," according to Rick, snickered about me: "I'm not going to see her face on the back of a milk carton, am I?" She referred to Rick as an "eyesore," but gave him work. We stayed with one of his coworkers. On payday, Rick walked into a bank to cash his check. I waited in the truck. A wrecker pulled in right behind me. I sat there alone in the parking lot not knowing what was going on. The guy got out of his rig and was using a payphone when Rick came out and saw that we were boxed in. He knew what was happening: the guy was trying to repossess our vehicle. Rick, using a jack, jacked up our truck, then shoved the rear end over as far as he could, which was only a foot or so. He did it several more times. Then, a lady walked to the car that was beside us. Flabbergasted at how someone would block us in like they did, she started her car and pulled out. Foot by foot, Rick inched our way to freedom.

Not wanting to lose our ride, Rick decided we'd leave Sacramento and head farther south. Our first stop was in Atascadero, where one of his two sons lived. Rick had no contact with either of his children and spoke very little to me of the circumstances surrounding why. The son in Atascadero was a freshman in high school; the other (location unknown) had, according to Rick, already graduated. Without so much as the courtesy of a heads-up to the mother, we stopped in at his youngest son's home. The boy wasn't there and wasn't expected back until the following day. Rick described his son's mother as "high maintenance," yet I sensed he had a strong connection with her. She invited us to spend the night and stayed up late talking with Rick while I tried to get some rest on her couch. As they gave Dude, Rick's Pomeranian, a bath in the kitchen sink, I overheard her inquiring about our relationship. In so many words, Rick painted her a picture of rescuing a helpless victim from the horrors of a place called Concow. When she asked him how he felt about me, his answer was, "I'm content." That was nice to overhear, given that there was a pretty good chance I was pregnant.

The next day, again without permission, Rick dropped in at his son's football practice. This upset the mother. On her way to work, wearing a cute navy-blue dress with white polka dots, she told Rick that if I needed help, she would help me; otherwise, we had to go.

Rick and I headed south until we reached where "normal, civilized people lived," his old stomping ground—Ventura County. During the day, he hit up construction outfits for drywall finishing jobs; during the night, we slept in the back of his pickup at rest areas. In Ojai, he found work. We stayed with another coworker of his, for about a month, until Rick began moving in on the coworker's household—sitting in *his* chair and even getting a little too friendly with his wife—and we were asked to leave.

Finally, in Oxnard, we moved into a two-bedroom duplex by the beach. We shared it with a guy named Red. An alcoholic, Red looked just like Yosemite Sam, mustache and all. I contacted Mom again to let her know I was okay and this time where I was. Lori asked to come visit us for a few days; I knew that was to check on me. She did and, before she left, we made sure to take advantage of the gorgeous beach along the Pacific Ocean.

Rick and I had barely gotten settled into our duplex when he started going to bars all the time and not returning home until after closing. His attitude and tone turned gruff. Confused, I felt that familiar "unwanted" feeling, like I was a burden. Now certain I was pregnant, I lay in our bed alone night after night crying about my predicament. To my relief, around the end of my first trimester, Rick asked me if I wanted to go back home. I needed my mom; I said yes.

———

In January of 1988, on a cold day in Concow, I sat on that same brown vinyl couch with the worn-out cushions that I had wanted so badly to get away from. To my surprise, there were no signs of meth anywhere. I knew I had hurt my mom. We both knew that there was no way to undo the damage I had done. Warming herself in front of the wall heater, she said, "Billy Jack's really disappointed in you. I told him, 'Jenny's just taking the long road, but she'll get there.'" Mom did seem to have my back at times, even when I didn't deserve it.

Rick was good at finding jobs, just not keeping them. He'd land one, work a week or two, until he was paid, then not show up on Monday. Until we could rent our own place, Rick and I stayed with his friends Sid and Lisa. Sid, like Rick, was a drinker. When they consumed alcohol together, things got crazy. They'd compete in poker, darts, and gambling until they couldn't stand each other anymore. During Super Bowl XXII, they got drunk and argued to the point of wrestling over the game on the living room floor. With his head, Sid knocked out four of Rick's upper front teeth. They were laughing about it while it happened. I took a walk down Concow Road to an old friend's house, because I had nowhere else to go. *What had I done to my life?*

Rick and I moved out of Sid and Lisa's and into a double-wide trailer. The rent was a pricy $600 a month, but it was spacious and nice. While I was down south, Lori had taken what she wanted of my personal items from my old bedroom—including my graduation dress! I got it and some other things back, the most important being a small box of my family's photographs. I was the keeper of the pictures. With the items I had available to me, I decorated our home, which turned out to be cute.

Rick continued to stay at the bars, most often the Rock House in Concow, until closing time and began threatening me when he got home. He'd viciously snarl: "You won't be taking my kid from me."

I hadn't even given birth yet, and I had no idea why he'd say that. Intimidated and scared, I'd respond: "I wouldn't do that to you."

"Good."

We didn't live alone long because Sid and Lisa separated, so Sid moved in with us. That helped with furnishings, half of the rent, and perhaps kept Rick's threats at bay.

Before I knew it, given Rick's lousy work ethic, I was sixteen, pregnant, and sitting in the welfare office waiting for my name to be called—somewhere I thought I'd never be. When the money came in every month, I took control of it and put it where it was supposed to go, unlike Mom and Billy Jack used to do. Surprisingly, Rick was fine with me handling the funds; the less responsibility he had, the happier he was. I sat through the WIC—Women, Infant, and Children—appointments for the free food vouchers. Other moms often threw out the f-bomb because they had to attend nutritional and parenting classes, but I enjoyed them. I wanted to learn how to become a good mother.

Rick's truck, the *wanted* one, we deemed repo-ed when it went missing. When he couldn't take me to one of my obstetrician appointments because we had no vehicle, I had to ask Mom and Billy Jack. On the way, I rode with my rear passenger window down and head against the door frame to breathe clean air rather than their marijuana smoke. I remember wondering if the doctor was going to smell it on me. He didn't mention it if he did. I insisted that Rick find a way to drive me to future visits, even if he had to borrow my parents' car. When I'd left Concow initially with him, I'd left all substances behind—marijuana, booze, tobacco. And determined to bring a healthy baby into the world, my unborn child wasn't going to be exposed to anything harmful—not even caffeine. When Mom noticed my commitment, she commented that my trying so hard made her worried something might go wrong. I guess I worried, too. Mom started doing her part to not subject me to her and Billy Jack's smoke.

Five months after coming back home and fifteen hours of labor, Dr. Fillerup delivered not Tiffany Jean, but Zack "the Lego maniac" as we called him. My incredible little miracle weighed a whopping nine pounds, four-and-a-half ounces. I was proud, as was Rick. The day after our child was born, Rick brought me a flower picked from someone's yard. He used a soda bottle for a vase.

At home, I cried as I stood and looked in the mirror at what my young body had gone through to create a life. I was told it would go back. Essentially a child myself, Zack was my little towhead, and he was worth it. I renewed my determination and refused to raise my son the way I had been raised: in an environment filled with drugs, dysfunction, and destitution.

CHAPTER SEVEN

THE CRÈME DE LA CRÈME

When I stepped into my room at the Marriott,
I threw open the curtains to see what the world
looked like from something other than ground
floor in the boonies...

Sid reunited with Lisa and moved out. That left Rick and me with the full monthly rent of $600. I was staring into our empty refrigerator when Rick handed me forty dollars for diapers *and* groceries. *Really? Are you kidding?* I didn't have the guts to say it out loud. That was the moment I realized it would be up to me to support us. Zack was just two months old when I signed up for independent study through the high school. I'd do my coursework at home, then Rick would drop Zack and me off at school, where I'd take weekly tests. Having to depend on Rick for rides got old. It took me three tries to pass the written DMV driver's license test, but I finally did. I drove a 1971 green Dodge

Coronet that we bought from Sid for $100. It was an ugly "tank" with a ripped interior headliner that flapped around if the windows were down, but it got me where I needed to go.

Unable to make the rent on our double-wide, we moved into a dumpy tiny travel trailer that had a room added on to it. That was only $100 a month, which included utilities. Still, we struggled financially. With a young child, I wasn't getting through school very fast. It would have taken me two years to get where I needed to be right at that moment: employable. I decided to take the GED test. Because I was under eighteen, I had to get special permission from the superintendent of the school district. During our meeting, I told him my plan: first pass the GED, then attend Butte Community College. He sat back in his chair for a few moments to think about it, and then he said, "With a GED and a two-year degree, you'll be fine." That was the answer I needed. I studied for the test the best I could with an infant. When it finally rolled around, it was easier than I had expected. I was a slow reader, but I passed on the first try. I was on my way.

While I was busy bettering myself for my family, Rick was busy learning about Billy Jack's fighting chickens. Soon they were staked out and in pens at our house, too. Rick wanted to breed, sell, and, of course, fight them. He loved to gamble, no matter what game it was. I abhorred it but didn't have any say. I was at home with six-month-old Zack one afternoon when a man showed up at our door looking for Rick. He was inquiring about a rooster. I told him Rick wasn't around and I wasn't sure when he'd be back. Audaciously, the man strolled right into our backyard, grabbed a rooster, and left with it. When Rick returned, I told him what had happened. It must have chafed his ego, because he and Sid went over to Mom and Billy Jack's, where the man was, to confront him. A fight ensued inside my parents' house, and the man stabbed Rick seven times. Sid raced Rick to the hospital, where surgeons did emergency exploratory surgery. Later Rick said the guy must have been on meth because "he just wouldn't go down." I laughed when Rick justified the confrontation by saying that the man had "made Jenny cry." I only cried when I was stuck taking care of Rick and read the headline on the front page of the newspaper: "Concow Man Stabbed in Dispute over Chicken."

The owner of our rental was an elderly woman who didn't want "trouble," so she evicted us. We moved into a single-wide trailer with Sid and Lisa that sat atop a mountain on twelve beautiful acres. Our roommates soon bought a house in town, and we took over the rent. The payment was a mere $100 per month (again), but this property was priceless. From the added-on knotty pine living room's bay window, I could see over the entire city of Oroville. If the clouds were low, it looked as if I could walk right out onto them. And at night, there were millions of tiny stars. Just outside our living room door was a tree that birds loved. When a baby blue jay fell out of its nest, I rescued it. "Jay" would fly from his birdcage across the room to my finger to retrieve nightcrawlers. I usually left his cage door open, and one day he flew away through an open window. Thereafter, he'd hang out in the tree from which he had originally fallen. Sometimes wild animals made it to the top near our home, like a bear that tried to get into Rick's chicken pens when he was gone. I thought I'd scare it off with a .22 rifle, but every time I'd pull the lever back, a shell would pop out of the side. Like our spacious double-wide trailer, I loved this home, but not Rick's drinking and verbal abuse, which had gotten worse.

I'd acquired my GED and driver's license, but I desperately needed skills to land a job and earn some money, so Butte College was next. I enrolled for the upcoming semester in general education courses and a beginning typing class. I did the best I could juggling school and a toddler. Even in college I was afraid to speak up or sit in the front of the classroom, but I really enjoyed learning. Every paper I had to write was related to my son: how to instill values in children; how to raise respectful, successful young men. Zack was my motivation. I wanted to give him a good life. Most of all, I wanted him to have a mom he could be proud of.

With financial aid, nominal money from my cleaning houses, Pell Grants, Board of Governors Fee Waivers, and book vouchers, I stayed afloat. When my student loan came in, I got rid of my ugly "tank" and bought our neighbor's Toyota Tercel, named the "Zipper." It had a manual transmission, so I had to learn to drive a stick, but once I did, I was off. I drove the Zipper for a year, then sold it for more than I'd paid. I then bought a Toyota Celica. Rick wrecked it while drunk. I got another student loan and a nearly identical car, eventually ending up in a burgundy T-top Camaro. Rick was approved for the Supplemental Security Income, SSI, benefits he'd applied for after he was stabbed and planned to buy his own pickup truck with the backpay, but before it happened, Mom and Billy Jack's car broke down, so they asked me for a ride. Of course, I said yes. When we reached their destination across town, just like old times, Billy Jack walked into a house, Mom and I sat in the car talking, then Billy Jack emerged carrying a brown paper bag of marijuana. I couldn't believe it. I didn't want to be part of a drug deal—or transport pot, which was illegal, with my car. Fuming mad, I said, "Mom, I can't do this anymore."

She said, "I know."

The older I got, the bolder I became toward Rick, too. He still justified our relationship to others by saying he rescued me—in my presence—like I was some sort of stray. That was hard for me to hear, and when I'd heard enough, I'd let him have it. Once I threw Zack's baby bottle at him but missed and hit a fish tank, sending a wall of water onto the floor of Sid and Lisa's living room. On a camping trip down at POE Powerhouse, I was so fed up with Rick's blather about rescuing me that, with "Guitar Larry" strumming the Marshall Tucker Band song "Can't You See" in the background, I grabbed his beer from between his legs and slowly poured it over his head. As it dripped down his face and onto his lap, he just sat there with his drunken smile. I'm sure the others appreciated that I had put a cork in it.

One night, he came home from the bar completely smashed and ripped Zack out of my arms. He said, "If you take him from me, I'll be able to find you. You'll have to be on welfare. You'll have to have a PG&E bill. I'll find you, and I'll take Zack across the border to Mexico. You'll never see him. Or, if I can't find you, I'll kill everyone in your family, except for your mom, because I like her. I'll kill all of your nieces and nephews—everyone."

I jumped out of bed and got right back in his face: "You'll never take him away from me. He is mine. You are shit!"

He kicked me in my ribs, cracking one, and I went flying back onto the bed. The next day he apologized, like he always did, and when he hugged me, I felt the rib shift back into place. I also had a nice shoeprint bruise directly under my breast. I never jumped in his face again.

With two semesters of college under my belt—English, typing, health, office administration, computer science (in lieu of public speaking)—I was starting up my third when I overheard a teacher mention the new court reporting program. I wondered if that was the same thing as a stenographer, which Mom and Billy Jack had suggested I become years earlier during my family's pipe dream powwow. I asked and was told that it was. After a few more questions, the next thing I knew, I was switching my classes around. It was too late to enroll in the very first court reporting class at the college, but I rearranged some things and set myself up for the second the following semester. Luckily, all the classes I'd already taken were part of the two-year court reporting program. However, to make it to state licensure, I had to build my shorthand speed to over two hundred words a minute, and that could take longer than two years. I knew it wouldn't be easy, but I was excited. At orientation, official court reporters spoke to our group, and one said, "As soon as you get licensed, go out and max out that credit card on some work clothes, because you'll be able to pay it off!"

Spring 1991, I was part of "Class 02." The opposite of composers—creating notes from sounds rather than sounds from notes—we court reporting students were the "crème de la crème." At least that's how the short, round, red-headed program coordinator addressed us. To get started, I bought an old secretarial shorthand machine for $175. The tray held only a half of a pad of steno paper, but the machine was tough. Mid-semester, several students received brand new machines through PIC, the Private Industry Council. After contacting PIC, by way of trading in my old one, I received one, too, a brand new $4,000 burgundy Stentura 6000. It was the perfect tool to help my fingers fly.

The first semester was spent learning the basics of machine shorthand, or Theory I, which was like a completely new language. The daytime classroom hours were long and arduous, then there was speed-building practice at home during the evenings. It was challenging, but I loved it. Rick still drank, but he started being nice and supportive of me; probably because I now had a future. I became pregnant with our second son. Rick and I got wedding rings and planned to marry sometime down the road. Carrying nineteen course units, I made honor roll that semester.

The second semester was spent learning advanced machine shorthand, or Theory II, and speed building. By fall, I was right on track at 100 words per minute. I did get stuck there, a "plateau" as it's called, but was assured by the teacher, "This too shall pass," which it did.

Rick's niceness and supportiveness didn't last, however. I'd go to school during the week and spend Saturday and Sunday cleaning houses, mowing lawns, and/or gardening—anything for milk and gas. When I was out being responsible, he'd run around Concow. When I'd get home, he'd drop Zack with me and take off again. Once, after cleaning a house, I handed him $20.00 to fill up the propane tank so I could take a hot shower. He made it home after closing time, empty-handed.

In December of 1991, Rick was out late at the bar; I was at home asleep, due to have our child in three days. I heard a knock on the door. It was our neighbor, Korbin.

"Jenny, Rick's been in an accident. He hit a tree and he's messed up pretty bad."

My niece Amber, now eleven, had been staying with Rick and me. She looked after Zack until Mom picked them up minutes later; Korbin and I hurried to the grisly scene on Big Bend—a windy road that's everything its name implies. Rick had been on his way home, damn fast apparently, when he wrapped his pick-up—the one he bought with his SSI settlement—around a large pine tree. The entire left side of his body was mangled: upper arm broken, shattered kneecap. The left side of his face was torn off in a flap across his eye. Korbin and I got him out of his driver's seat and into the passenger seat of my Camaro. When I reached down to shift the car into drive, I accidentally grabbed his knee without a kneecap. It was an eerie feeling. When we made it to the hospital, he was transported by ambulance to an emergency trauma center in the next town, where he was admitted. A nurse handed me a plastic bag containing the bloody clothing they had cut off Rick's body; the only thing in my mind was death.

Brooke spent the night at my house on my due date, and sure enough, I went into labor. She and my mom stayed with me through delivery. Four hours after the first contraction, there he was at nine pounds with a full head of black hair. Was this my child? Zack was a towhead, but this one looked Mexican. Searching for a name, I thought he looked like an "Anthony." Brooke brought a picture of him to Rick in the next town. Via a phone call, before I had a chance to suggest the name "Anthony," Rick said, crunching Frosted Flakes, "How about Tony? Tony the Tiger." So, we named him Anthony; Tony for short.

As soon as I was released from the hospital, Rick insisted on being released, too. I slept on the living room sofa with my toddler and newborn; Rick was in a hospital bed next to us. If the boys weren't waking me in the night, their father was. I was beyond exhausted. Brooke and Korbin helped during the day as best they could; Amber every second she wasn't in school. Grandma Maggie, all the way from Stockton, also showed up to assist.

Rick's face had been deformed in the wreck, and he was in a lot of pain. His anger turned to rage. Bedridden at first, he would yell and complain day in and day out. When he could use his wheelchair, his attitude was no better; he was still helpless. One night, his chickens started squawking in distress. He demanded that I go out to check on them, but it was pitch black, so I refused. He was irate. The next day, the chickens went off again when I wasn't home. While sitting in his wheelchair, he shot his rifle straight through the roof of our trailer to scare whatever it was away.

Rick recuperated, progressing from the wheelchair to a cane, and when he got back on his feet completely, he started drinking and closing the bars again. Until he finagled his own rig, I'd have to pick him up in the middle of the night. Rick was out when Brooke stopped by to visit. She said she'd spoken with a girl my age named Darcy, and that Darcy told her she had "partied" with Rick at the Rock House, implying that he'd cheated on me with her. I knew he had in the past—like with the prostitute that ended up in his room during his stay in Reno. "She stole my wallet and left me a cigarette, but I didn't have sex with her." *Liar*. I knew he hit on other women, and I sensed the looks people gave me about my pitiful situation. It didn't bother me that he had cheated, because after his wreck I was done with him and his destructive lifestyle. I wanted out, and as soon as possible. Besides, I was later able to use the Darcy incident to justify a precarious situation I put myself in.

I pressed on in school. In the spring of 1992, I passed 120 words per minute, then 140, where I plateaued again. It wasn't until the following spring—a whole year—that I managed to pass 160 and 180. I was almost at the 200 speed that I needed to qualify for the state exam, become licensed, get a job, and get out. Then depression and my worst fear, being alone, set in. If I did complete school and leave Rick, with two kids already, nobody would ever love me again. Plus, leaving Rick meant I'd have to leave my boys, or else he'd take them from me and out of the country. Zack and Tony were all I had. What was the point in being free without my kids? Feeling afraid, that summer I found the courage to make a call.

Jonny's mother answered. "Hello?"

"Is Jonny there?"

"Just a minute."

"Hello?" It was Jonny.

"Hi," I said in an awkward tone of voice.

"Who is this?"

"Jennifer."

"How are you? Are you okay?"

"Yeah. How are you?"

"I'm all right. What's going on?" After a pause, "So I hear you have a couple of kids now."

"Yes, I do."

Sounding perplexed, "Jennie-fer, why are you calling me?"

"I don't know. Just to see how you're doing, I guess."

"I still love you."

"I love you, too. I better go."

"Okay."

After that call, I'd tell Rick that I was going to school, but instead drop by Jonny's house. He was back—clean, drug-free. We would hang out and watch music videos, talk, tickle, tease, and laugh. He still looked at me in a way that's hard to explain, but it was warm and didn't take anything away from me. I loved being with him, and I felt it was mutual. Once his mom was there, too. Seated comfortably across the room from Jonny and me, she seemed to enjoy my company and showed interest in the court reporting program that I was in. One of Aaron Neville's videos came on the television and she said, "I don't know why he doesn't get that mole removed from above his eye, because he's not a bad-looking man." One time, when Jonny and I were alone, "Runaway Train" came on and he said, "You know, this song has helped a lot of runaways turn around and go home."

I didn't know what to say except, "Oh. Yeah."

I managed to sneak in a total of three "outings" to Jonny's. During the first, I got my one-and-only no-seatbelt ticket driving to his house. The second, Rick showed up at the college looking for me because Zack fell off a couch and had to have stitches above his eye. I wasn't there. I gave him a bogus story when I got home. It's not like he had never given me one before. Besides, what about Darcy? The last, Jonny asked if I wanted to see his place.

"Sure."

He showed me the kitchen, bathroom, his parents' bedroom, and then he showed me his bedroom. He stepped inside. I cautiously stayed by the doorjamb. He pointed to his bowling trophies and awards and pictures of himself. His room was organized and clean, and his waterbed was tightly made.

"And there's my waterbed," he said, in what I took as an invitation. My heart sank as we made eye contact.

"I better go."

"Okay."

I gathered my purse and made it to the front door. He hugged me and tried to give me a full-on kiss goodbye. I just couldn't, though, because I knew what would happen to me if Rick found out: I would be dead meat. I vanished and ended all contact with Jonny.

I tried the straightforward approach with Rick: "We need to talk. I don't want to be with you anymore. I love someone else." He grabbed his keys and left, returning after the bar closed. In his drunken ruthlessness, he threatened to take my boys and kill my family until I gave in and said I wanted to stay. I had opened a dangerous door—he knew I wanted out—and it was clear that he wasn't going to let me go. Returning home to Mom and Billy Jack's wasn't an option for me. Number one, because Rick often hung out there and, as he threatened, he would kill them. Number two, they had a houseful with my nieces and nephews. Number three, I wasn't subjecting my sons to their lifestyle any more than necessary.

I found a counselor that accepted Medi-Cal. Rick and I tried that together. At the beginning of the two sessions we made it through, the counselor set his kitchen timer. After each forty-five minutes of getting nowhere, it went off: "Oh, your time is up." That wasn't going to work. It was hopeless. The only way out was to finish school and get a job.

I buckled down in speed-building class and that fall passed 200 words per minute, then the "qualifier," the test that permits you to take the test of all tests, the state exam. It would be held in November at the Marriott in Burlingame, California.

Rick took me to the grocery store parking lot where I met my ride to the city. I kissed my boys goodbye and loaded my bag into my classmate's car; she was heading to the state exam as well. Rick stood holding Tony in one arm and holding Zack's hand with the other as we pulled away.

When I stepped into my room at the Marriott, I threw open the curtains to see what the world looked like from something other than ground floor in the boonies. It was amazing! I went down to the restaurant where I enjoyed a nice dinner that included a cranberry sunrise cocktail, as I was twenty-two now, amid an elegant view of the bay as the sun set. I went to bed early, as the first part of my exam was scheduled for 8:00 a.m. sharp.

The next morning, I went down to check in for the test. It was all new to me, and I felt out of place, but I had to pass through "here" to get to "there." I felt awkward, too, because everyone was in jeans and sweats—comfortable clothing—while I was in three-inch heels and a green rayon dressy pant suit. Obviously, I'd had no idea what to expect. One of the girls from my group made a roundabout comment about people being dressed up for the test: "Who are they trying to impress?" My classmate smiled at me; I didn't say a word.

The machine shorthand dictation portion was held in a conference room set up as a mock trial. It consisted of a panel of four people at the "judge's bench" with a placard to designate "The Court," both the plaintiff and defense attorneys, and then the witness. To pass this part of the exam we had to take down ten minutes of dialogue at 200 wpm with an accuracy of 97.5 percent or better.

8:00 a.m. rolled around before I knew it. Maybe it was because I was naive, but I went into the testing room feeling extremely confident. During the beginning of the dictation, I was keeping up. In fact, I was nailing it. Then, about halfway in, I lost all focus. I went from knowing "I have this" to my hands scrambling for words in mush. I wasn't breathing and started to panic. I stroked "garbage notes," as we called it, for the entire second half of the test. I exited the exam room, trying to hold back my tears, and went to the transcription room. I started typing, hoping it wouldn't be as bad as I thought, but I could see exactly where I fell apart and knew it was a total loss. I didn't even finish typing it up, just turned in what I had completed and walked out to be alone in my room. Only offered twice a year, once in the spring and once in the fall, I knew I would have to wait six months to take the dictation portion of the test again. I trudged on through the written ones—English and Professional Practices—and did the best I could.

When the results arrived in the mail several weeks later, they confirmed my gut feeling that I hadn't passed any of the sections on the test and I'd be going back to school to prepare for the next exam six long months down the road. I didn't think I could wait another six months.

In an attempt to leave Rick, I secretly rented a small trailer that was right next to its owner's house. With somebody nearby, I was hoping to feel safe. When Rick found out about it, he was clearly upset, but he acted like he had no choice and played along. After I, with my boys, spent the day moving in, I delivered them to Rick, as he insisted. He showed right up at my trailer. Five-year-old Zack had managed to direct him to where I lived. I knew I wouldn't be safe, so I packed up my stuff without a fight and went back with my head down.

My inability to be free from Rick caused me to fall into another, much deeper, depression. I barely made it to school. I didn't want to die, but I didn't want to live anymore either. I fantasized about swerving my Camaro into the lane of a big rig, just to end it all. But I couldn't do that to my boys. At rock bottom, I sought help. At just twenty-two years old, with two young kids, I opened the phone book to find someone to talk to. I found a Christian psychologist in town. I suppose I felt that was a safe place. Life must have beaten me into submission, though, because I could barely speak when I made the call. The receptionist answered and explained that Tim, the counselor, didn't accept Medi-Cal, but did accept payment on a sliding scale. I really wanted an appointment, but a telephone appointment. Not in person. I was too ashamed of myself and my choices.

"Can I just talk to him over the phone?"

Delicately, she said, "Usually he likes to have the first session in person. Can I have him call you?"

I mumbled, "Okay."

Tim called and, after much persuasion, I agreed to an in-person appointment.

The office was a cottage-style house in a residential neighborhood and painted in one of my favorite color combinations—burgundy and blue. As I walked in, there was a matching couch and loveseat with coordinating pillows. In the corner was an antique wooden phone booth. Was Tim supposed to be Superman? Was this where ET phones home? Was this where you enter—or leave—*The Twilight Zone*? There was an Ansel Adams photograph hanging on the wall and a vase full of flowers on the coffee table that was neatly organized with magazines. On the floor was a basket full of kids' books with *Where's Waldo* leaning upright against it. As I met Auriga, a German Shepherd, I could hear the soft sound of oldies playing in the background.

When it was time for my session, Tim came out and introduced himself. He was very tall and had hair just above his shoulders. He was attired in a buttoned shirt with the sleeves rolled up, jeans, and expensive-looking leather boots. We walked in through the office area together and made a right turn. As we rounded the corner, there was an oak filing cabinet with a wooden "Imagine" sign on top of it. I later learned that John Lennon had been murdered on Tim's birthday, creating some sort of connection between the two, and that Tim was a huge fan of the Beatles.

He delivered me to the room and then turned around and walked out, leaving the door slightly ajar. I could hear him grinding coffee beans in what had once been the kitchen area of the house-turned-office. Separated by a large braided oval rug, I was seated on yet another couch across from a big oak desk. On the desk was a miniature Tin Man, like from *The Wizard of Oz,* and books. On the wall above were Tim's degrees, and the one from Butte College stood out from the rest because of the lighting. Later, he explained that he purposefully positioned it that way because that was where his life began to come together. (Several years after I first stepped into his office, he added a Ph.D. to the center of his layout.) To the left of the desk was a Tiffany-style lamp that hung above a tall, long-legged bird-like iron figurine named "Bill" that stood in the corner. There was a shelf full of psychology books with an acoustic guitar resting against it, and another oak filing cabinet. On the wall behind me was more Ansel Adams artwork.

At the start of the session, Tim greeted me with freshly brewed coffee, followed by tissue. Lots and lots of tissue. I noticed that he wasn't wearing a wedding band, which is something I tended to pick up on right away in a man. I remember trying to stereotype him as either a workaholic who didn't have time for a partner, a professional who liked to remain available, maybe he had a partner but didn't want to commit, or that he wasn't interested in women, period. The next session he had his wedding band on, though, and I learned that he was happily married with children. To add to my confusion, on the wall in a side room was a picture of a star within its galaxy that he said a *friend*—I presumed female—had bought for him. I was surprised that he had a wife *and* a (female) friend. Later I figured it was his wife who was his friend. Either way, that concept was entirely new to me.

One of Tim's first questions was, "How good are you at catching curveballs?"

It went right over my head.

Another, "Do you like music?"

"Yes."

"I mean good music?"

I answered again, "Yes."

"What's your favorite song?"

"A Murder of One" by the Counting Crows. It's on their *August and Everything After* CD." He gave me an odd look. I continued, "My favorite groups, though, are the Eagles and Aerosmith."

He said, "Well, the Eagles were good," then just rolled his eyes at me and started talking about Barbra Streisand and how she battled stage fright for years, and how Michael Bolton throws benefit concerts for abused women. Then he asked, "Do you like the acoustic or electric guitar?"

Without hesitation, I said, "The electric." This "girl with the long brown hair" had had her fill of heartache stemming from a certain musician and his acoustic guitar.

As I sat on his couch clenching the throw pillows, we touched upon Rick, Zack and Tony, and my schooling. There was so much on my plate, I didn't know where to start. I just wanted to bang my head against the wall because I couldn't make sense of anything. I cried during every single session for weeks. Honestly, I don't know how he tolerated me.

Early on in therapy, I brought up my relationship with Jonny. "Where is he right now?"

"I don't know. He's probably sleeping; he sleeps all day."

Tim thought Jonny was a bad idea and said something about soul mates. "You're not the same person you were back then," he told me. Also, "If you don't do the hard work of becoming whole on your own, all of your relationships will fall disappointingly flat." He went on to say, "Ask your friends; they'll tell you what you should do about him."

I didn't really have any friends besides Brooke, and she couldn't help me. I didn't have family to guide me either. I wasn't his typical client.

Trying to find something for me to hang on to, he asked, "Didn't you ever go to church?"

I replied, "No, not really. Well, maybe once," as I vaguely recalled stepping into one and watching baptisms.

Surprised at my answer, he said, "Some people say you have to see it to believe it. I say you have to believe it to see it." Then he asked me about going to group counseling.

"I can't do group counseling. There's no way. I'm too shy."

"My theory of being shy is it is just a feeling of inadequacy."

I shook my head.

I brought my boys in with me to the next two sessions. I was proud to show them off. In hindsight, though, it was also a way for me to hide behind them and not deal with the real issues. Tim suggested they go to a sitter, if possible. As we continued in therapy alone together, I couldn't get past being uneasy around him. He addressed my wall of "don't let my guard down because I'll be preyed upon by yet another man" with a simple "I'm not vulnerable." I remember thinking, *That's odd*.

Tim accepted as little as $20 a session in the beginning. If I didn't have the cash, he would hold checks for me until Friday, when I'd get paid for cleaning houses. Sometimes the checks would bounce, and I'd have to catch up. It was a mess. Finally, regarding finances, he asserted, "I am a priority." I understood. Payments were thereafter made on time. I had no idea that was the beginning of a very long professional relationship. As I progressed, so did the price, which was fair.

Eventually Tim invited Rick in with us. As soon as Tim called him on some of his behaviors, Rick became so angry and defensive that he walked out of the office and left, peeling away in my Camaro. Tim felt he was dangerous and, knowing I wanted out of the relationship, suggested I leave town. But I couldn't leave; I had nowhere to go. Plus, technically, I was still in school. Tim was clear: "You have to protect yourself." He could have been Clint Eastwood when he glanced over at the bottom drawer of his desk, intimating that that was where he housed his pistol, and said, "I protect myself." I don't really know if he kept a pistol in there, but I got his point.

Rick hated that I went to counseling, but, aside from the painful work I was doing in there, I loved it. I finally had somebody in my corner. I had hope. At the end of each session, I'd raise the hood on my Camaro, reach in, and start it. Rick had hotwired my car after the inside ignition went out. Tim would stand, watching from his front door, as if to say, *Wow*...

The second state exam was at the Marriott in Los Angeles. That was the first time I had ever been to L.A., and the first time I had been on an airplane. Like a kid on a thrill ride in a theme park, I loved the flight. The first evening at the Marriott, I used a gift certificate from our teacher for a session with a hypnotist specifically for court reporter examinees. It was supposed to help with test anxiety. Right in the middle of the tranquility, as I lay peacefully with fellow test takers, the hotel room's phone rang and startled everybody from our enchantment. The hypnotist was perturbed. I still felt quite relaxed when I left. In fact, the next day when I took the dictation test, I was completely relaxed, like passing didn't matter at all. My fingers worked almost in slow motion and wouldn't move fast enough, but I was getting it—well, most of it. I was slow and steady, steady and slow, but no, it wasn't a go. I did manage to make it through the entire test, though, even typing it all up. Progress, I guess. The following day, I took both written portions of the exam and felt a little bit better about them than I had the first time.

Several weeks later, I received the results in the mail. This time I learned that I had passed the English portion. That meant

I was back in school again to prepare for the next exam six more long months down the road. Again, I didn't know if I could wait that long.

I tried leaving Rick again and stayed a week at my stepsister's house. I should have stuck it out but didn't. Rick hooked up with an old friend of mine from high school. I became jealous or insecure, I'm not sure which, and went back to him. After the fact, it hit me that he was trying to do exactly that, make me jealous or insecure, and it had worked.

Disappointed, Tim asked, "And what was your favorite movie again?"

"Forrest Gump."

"And who do you relate to? Jenny or Forrest?"

I came back at him with, "Who do you think?" But the truth was that I had to stop and consider it for a minute.

My relationship with Rick wasn't getting any better. He started harassing me about school: "You're going five years to a two-year college." Or, "You just want a young attorney in a Bimmer." And his drunken rage was so much worse. If I did something he didn't like, he'd make an X on the calendar and say, "Strike one! At strike three, you're out!" He'd walk into the house and tell me that I had five minutes to gather my things, to leave the boys, and "get the fuck out." When I'd start to leave, he'd have the spark plug wires crossed or the coil unplugged on my car. After closing the bar down one night, he climbed into our bed wanting to have sex. I wasn't interested. He became irate and started yelling and threatening me. I got so scared that I ran outside in my panties and hid behind a tree in the dark until he passed out. Rick intimated to me one afternoon that he was going to kill himself. He grabbed his pistol and walked out of the house to his pickup, where he sat alone. After an hour or more, I heard a gunshot. I didn't even bother to check on him. He came in later that night mad that I didn't care.

Rick's and my tumultuous relationship continued, but I stayed in school and in counseling. Tim spent months trying to "rewire my hard drive," as he'd say, and doing his best to imbed his wisdom: "Keep your blinders on, Jenny"—as a horse does to stay on track. He once asked, "Do you follow your heart or your head?" I'm still trying to figure that one out. My head said go, but my heart was afraid. When you're the first in your family to go to college and strive for a better life, it can feel like you're leaving everyone behind. Tim invested a lot of time in teaching me that it was okay to move beyond my family of origin. He gave me a glimpse of the perks of hard work by letting me sit in the passenger seat of his BMW—with the door open and my shoes on—and showing off his killer stereo system. His encouragement helped. I plugged along toward my goal of having a good job so I could take care of my boys and myself.

Brooke's grandma had a room for rent, so I took advantage of the opportunity and left Rick again. I hoped he would eventually let go, but instead, he continued to harass and call me names. He would sit with our kids and pray, "Please bring Mommy back home to us." Still, I tried for things to be amicable. I accepted an invitation from him for dinner with the boys at his house. In the middle of eating, he said, "Scruffy's gone. I had to kill her because she kept leading Zack off into the woods."

Scruffy was our dog. Feeling sick to my stomach, I left.

Within days of the Scruffy incident, I had to drop the boys off with Rick at his house. I drove there not knowing what I was getting into, because I never knew what to expect with him. When I pulled into the driveway, he took the boys out of the car, closed the door, and opened and closed the trunk as if he had put something in there. He then started talking about a pipe bomb and saying, "I'm sorry, Jenny. I'm so sorry." I found myself in a state of mind that's hard to explain; like a trance. Emotionally, I was shut down; prepared to die at any moment. And I didn't care whether I lived or died, I just wanted to get away from him. Somberly, I drove off thinking any second my car was going to blow up. If it did, it would have been worth it at that time.

While we were separated, one of Rick's acquaintances asked him for my telephone number. That didn't help matters. Rick kicked him in the groin and tried to gouge out his eyes. Shortly thereafter, I arrived home at Brooke's grandma's. Rick was waiting at the gate for me. What started out with him asking where I had been turned into an argument and him pulling my hair through my car's window. Then he sped off.

The upshot was when he showed up at my house at five in the morning, checking to see if I had a man with me. There was no man. We got into another argument. It escalated to the point that he pulled out his .25 and, aiming right for the gas tank, shot my car. The bullet didn't penetrate the body, luckily. Hysterical, I ran down the road to the first house I could hide in, but nobody was home. I can't remember how, maybe I hitchhiked, but

I ended up in the Concow School parking lot speaking to a policeman. Rick was arrested.

The day Rick was released from jail, I was on my way to Marine World with the boys and my niece Sam, Lori's daughter. I passed him standing barefoot at the intersection of Highway 70 and Table Mountain Boulevard. He was hitchhiking in the opposite direction, back up the hill. He tried to flag me down, but I just kept on going. In my rear-view mirror, I saw him yelling at the top of his lungs. I knew I would have to eventually come back home, but the kids and I had a much-needed day away.

When I returned, Brooke's grandma wanted me to get a restraining order against Rick. I was too afraid to, so she told me I had to move. With a bag of our clothes and my shorthand machine in its case, my boys and I hid at Sid and Lisa's house until I could get into the Catalyst Shelter for Battered Women. I slept on their living room floor, secreted between the coffee table and couch. Had I slept on the couch, Rick could have driven by and seen me through their large front window. Tim kept telling me to leave town, but there was no way I could support my children, especially if I had to hide for the rest of my life. Once at Catalyst, I was among a houseful of strangers and, just like high school, I didn't fit in. I decided it was just too much for me. Who knows how long I would have had to stay there. I went back to Rick with my head down yet again, choosing to stay and finish school. Tim was beside himself.

The next exam was back at Burlingame. I rode along with my schoolmate just like before. This time I had only the Professional Practices and dictation portion to pass. After getting settled into the hotel room and studying hard, I went straight to bed. The next day I was confident as I walked into the testing room for the single written portion. During the exam, I knew most of the answers. The dictation test was the following day at 2:00 p.m., which just happened to be the exact time I normally took speed tests back at school. I knew that was in my favor. I walked into the dictation room, found my spot. I planted my feet firmly on the floor, sat squarely in my chair, forearms level, and reminded myself, "Remember to breathe." I also made a promise to God that if He would give the test to me that I would always give back—little gifts, like dropping change into the collection banks at the grocery store checkout line and the Salvation Army bowls at Christmastime, as well as anything else I was called to do. I promised, "I'll always be a giver." I was ready.

As the dictation started, I stroked diligently and deliberately, and I remembered to breathe. *I can do this.* There were rough spots, but I held on. When I'd start to lose focus, I'd come back through my breath. I made it all the way through to the end and transcribed that test with confidence. I proofread until the very last minute. I didn't know if I had passed or not, but I thought I had a good shot.

I anxiously awaited the results. Several weeks later, with Zack and Tony by my side at our rural mailbox in Concow, I opened the letter: "Congratulations on passing the CSR examination!" I grabbed my boys, and we raced back to the house. I kept reading it over and over to make sure I hadn't misread it. I showed it to Tim; I'm sure he was surprised. I was excited, because I knew my boys and I could now move forward, way over yonder, toward freedom, independence, and a comfortable life.

CHAPTER EIGHT

AN "INDEPENDENCE DAY" LIKE NO OTHER

*Rick fought dirty; I thought
I was going to die...*

Although being told, "The chances of getting a job around here are slim to zero," I received a call almost at once from a nearby deposition firm. With no money or credit, I didn't yet have the $4,000 computer and transcription software required to work. And, to make matters worse, I had been driving too fast in heavy rain on the freeway and hydroplaned my Camaro right into a brand-new minivan that still had the dealer plate. With a cracked frame, my car was totaled. Because carrying auto insurance was not yet mandatory, I had none...at all. When the driver of the minivan learned I had no coverage, he became quite furious—and animated. Lucky for me there was a highway patrolman on scene to keep him civil. I felt horrible and religiously made monthly installments to his insurance company until I paid off the $3,300 bill.

Hearing about my prospective job opportunity, Brooke's mom offered to charge my computer equipment to her credit card if I agreed to pay her back. I accepted with gratitude. As soon as the goods came in and the software was up and running, I was scheduled for my first deposition—wherein I'd report the out-of-court sworn testimony of witnesses—located at an attorney's office in Chico, CA, forty minutes away from Concow . Since I was without wheels, I had to borrow Mom and Billy Jack's car. That was a last resort given it was such an imposition for them to be without a vehicle during the workday, even though they didn't work. The third time I borrowed their car that week, Billy Jack extended his arm, turned his face away from me, and dropped the keys into my hand. Snidely, he said, "Here." I knew I wouldn't have access to their car much longer. Thankfully, a mechanic friend of Mom and Billy Jack's offered to help Rick fix my Camaro for free. They replaced the entire front clip and welded the frame where it was cracked. My car was now two-tone and a bit bowlegged, but I could get to and from my assigned depositions that were spread throughout Butte County.

First, I was assigned the easier depositions—traffic accidents and workers' comp claims—and then they put me on the harder jobs—heated divorce actions, multiple-attorney cases, and medical malpractice. I had to swear in witnesses—stumbling on the words of the oath for at least the first year—and mark and maintain exhibits. There was no judge; I was the one in charge. I gained a lot of useful experience, like learning the phonetic difference between "Waiting for Godot" and "Waiting for good dough." Editing that deposition transcript, I couldn't believe the defense attorney asked the plaintiff, "What, are you waiting for good dough?" even though it *was* a civil case. The attorney courteously called in for a correction to my transcript. That was embarrassing.

I loved having a job, and I loved getting paid. Within three months of starting work, I leased a brand-new Pontiac Grand Am with low payments. Life was looking good.

As luck would have it, however, Rick's and my landlady decided to clear cut all the trees on the property except for the four tall ones that were too close to our trailer. Just after Christmas 1995, a windstorm hit and kept Rick and me awake for most of the night. In the early morning, it grew so strong that, fearing for our safety, we gathered the boys and Amber, who was again staying with us, and hightailed it out of there. We returned before noon to find that the four trees had fallen like toy pick-up sticks on our home. One lay through the living room, smashing our Christmas tree that held Zack's and Tony's precious baby ornaments; two lay caved in on the bed we had been sleeping on; and one was across the back of my Camaro, having shattered the rear window. As I sifted through what was left of our life's belongings, fortunately, I found the most valuable things—the pictures—had been spared. We lived in a motel room until we could find another place, which turned out to be a double-wide trailer just down the road from our flattened one. It was newer and larger, but it lacked the awesome view over Oroville.

———

While I was taking the three CSR exams six months apart, Lori was finishing up a three-year sentence—for a meth-related offense—at the California Rehabilitation Center, a last option before prison. Prior to her release, she was moved to the House of Mercy, a transitional living facility. There, she found Christ and her most beautiful self. She felt loved, and it showed. Among my family, Lori was the first to get and stay clean from all substances. Underneath the layers of addiction was the most wonderful sister I could have asked for. Seeing the changes in her, I talked Teresa into giving the House of Mercy a try. When she agreed, I took a trip down to Stockton to pick her up, then delivered her there. Two days later, she bailed and hitch-hiked back to Stockton. All I could do was try.

Free from meth, Lori hooked up with Brooke's brother Seth, which I thought was crazy given she was a little older and a lot more experienced than he was, but it happened. In the formal ceremony she had dreamed of as a child, Lori—a stunning bride—married him. They moved into Brooke's now-deceased grandmother's house, the one I had lived in when Rick shot my car. There they had a son together, Preston, and took in Lori's other children—Sam, Stephanie, and Steven—whom Mom had been raising. Seth's mom lived down the road from him and his new wife, and Billy Jack and Mom, along with Teresa's two children, Stanley and Christina, had since moved in next door. I had my doubts about how the in-laws living in such close proximity was going to play out, but for the time being, all was right in Lori's world.

Solid in her recovery from meth, my sister and I enjoyed getting to know one another like never before. We often barbecued together and drank "Hop, Skip, and Go Nakeds" (a concoction of beer, lemonade, and tequila), and then walked down to Concow Lake where Lori swam in her bathing suit top or bra and shorts in the dark while I sat at the edge. After a dip in the water one evening, we were sharing stories of our crazy childhood when she said she'd always looked up to me.

"Why?" I asked.

"Because you're beautiful, you went to school, and"—with a heartfelt inflection in her voice—"everybody always loved you."

Sensing she hadn't felt loved in the same way that she assumed I had been, I replied, "Lori, you're beautiful, you can go to school and do anything you want, and everybody has always loved *you*, too."

After I'd finished school and obtained a job and a dependable vehicle, during one of Lori's and my get-togethers, she tattled, "Mom said you don't go around her and Billy Jack anymore because you're too good for everybody now that you have a job and a new car." So much for feeling loved. I was quite busy.

Within one of our more personal conversations, Lori told me she had been molested at eight years old. I felt that there was more that she wanted to say, but I didn't pry.

During another, I asked her about my real father, Ivan. The only thing she knew about him was that he and Mom were having sex when Mom went into labor with me. Lovely. So, unless Lori was confused, my biological father, Ivan, must have been the one who told Mom to call a cab at my birth.

The content of the conversations between my sister and me wasn't always what I wanted to hear, but our time together was golden.

Lori went on to enroll in college full time with the hope of becoming a probation officer. I wanted her to become one, too. On top of being an amazing wife, mother, and student, she eventually worked two jobs as well.

———

Ten years after first broaching the subject with Mom, I decided to ask her about my real father, Ivan, again. This time she gave me some names. I located Uncle George, who gave me Ivan's telephone number. When I called, a woman answered.

Nervously, I asked, "Is Ivan there?"

"No, not right now. Can I ask who is calling?"

"Jennifer."

Given her long pause, I felt she knew immediately who I was. She said she'd have him call me.

After several hours, my phone rang. I answered. "Hello?"

"Hi. Is this Jennifer?"

"Yes."

"It's Ivan, your father."

Throughout our rather brief discussion, we shed some tears, then arranged a time and place to meet. He and his wife, Pat, lived in Valley Springs, a mere thirty minutes east of the city where I'd resided until age thirteen, Stockton. He said he'd send me pictures of himself and Pat, which he did. On the back of his photo mailer he'd written, "I'm proud of you."

I was extremely anxious as Rick, the boys, and I pulled into Ivan and Pat's driveway. Once I was able to compose myself, we got out of the car to meet them. They stood up from the garage's table to greet us with hugs and tears. I could tell right away that they were Oakland Raiders die-hards because everything was decorated as such. And they were obviously heavy drinkers because there were cases of beer stacked by a trash can that was full of crushed empties waiting to be recycled. They were drinking when we arrived—and it was barely noon.

After pleasantries, the first comment out of my father's mouth was: "She's got her mother's ass." Pat maintained her smile without laughing at his remark.

Thanks, Dad.

When my father and I were alone, he expressed his take on Rick: "He should be a used-car salesman."

Here's another: "When I was with your mom, I was at the lowest point in my life."

As the day unfolded, Pat made sure—several times—to remind me, "Yep, I wrote out that child support check every month—one hundred dollars for Jennifer Seifert."

I took it all in and tried not to hold grudges.

Dad and Pat had a cozy home with pictures of their family covering the interior walls. They even had one of me that I had never seen. That was cool since I have maybe ten photographs of myself from my entire childhood. There were also pictures on their wall of my father's other daughters—Penny and Debbie—from his previous marriages. He said neither was in contact with him. I didn't ask why. *Wow*...I had two more older sisters. Mom had spoken of Debbie, but I'd had no idea about Penny, who looked like me. No other sibling did. Ivan didn't have Penny's telephone number, but he had Debbie's, and in the following weeks I reached out to her. I imagine my call caught her off guard, too, because she wasn't receptive.

My father dug out his old shoebox containing photographs of him, my late Aunt Virginia, Uncle George, and grandparents. Dad said my Grandpa George died in 1968 in a car wreck, when Dad was twenty-four. He was a tall, slender man with two wooden legs. He lost one leg while trying to jump a train and the other in a chainsaw accident. Grandma Zora died much later than Grandpa, in 1985, of diabetes. In the photos of her, I saw my nose and olive skin. My father laughed: "When my mom got mad at my dad, she'd hide his legs from him." I laughed, too. I learned that when Dad was nine, Grandma was driving drunk with him and his siblings in the car. She went off the road and over an embankment. The kids landed in the hospital; my father with a broken arm and a concussion. From the hospital, they landed in foster care, but were eventually returned home. As he spoke of it, I could tell he carried a lot of pain from that incident, and really from his entire alcohol-infused childhood. He closed the shoebox with the statement that he'd started drinking at just twelve years old.

Ivan hadn't been a dad to me, but I was willing to be the bigger person—as Mom always taught—and start anew. Sometimes it was tough, though, especially when after a few beers he'd say things like, "We made a will. You'd get more, but we're afraid your mother will get it." I wanted to fill a void, but not with his money.

———

Once I'd started bringing in a paycheck, Rick became nicer to me, that was true, but he also continued to drink, and I still wanted out. Even if he had quit alcohol and somehow turned into a perfect man, it wouldn't have mattered, too much bad stuff had happened between us. Plus, I wanted to feel love again—the kind of love I'd felt with Jonny. With a year of employment under my belt and the confidence that I could now support Zack, Tony, and myself, I secretly rented an apartment within a gated complex in town. On a morning when Rick was out and about in Concow, I called for Lori's help. We packed what we could of Zack's, Tony's, and my personal belongings into our vehicles. I left Rick a note.

On that "Independence Day," after unpacking the cars, I showed Zack and Tony their room. Lori and I sat on the living room floor of my empty apartment and shared a toast to freedom with an imaginary can of beer. I had made it out. Now was the hard part: staying out...and alive. Although the boys and I snuggled tight that night, it was, I felt, dreadfully cold.

Rick's countless threats, which had started during my pregnancy with Zack, about what would happen if I ever took his children from him were imprinted on my brain; the thought of doing that never crossed my mind. With a temporary restraining order in place, Rick and I exchanged the boys in the sheriff's department parking lot. I was quite liberal in giving him visitation with them—whenever he wanted it. I enrolled Zack in school in town and Tony in daycare, that way I could continue to work when I had them. *In propria persona*, I filed papers requesting only fifty-fifty joint physical and legal custody of our boys. The divorce attorney I sought out advised me that I would likely have to pay palimony to their father—unbelievable.

Rick fought dirty; I thought I was going to die. During one of the court hearings, he passed me a note threatening my life, but I was too afraid to tell anyone. He left the hearing before I did. When I arrived at my car, I found "HIV+" written on my license plate and a cut-up picture of me on the seat. I had the same feelings as on the day I thought he had put a pipe bomb in my trunk—whether I lived or not, I just wanted to be away from him. Somberly, I drove away.

The morning of the final custody hearing, all the years of domestic abuse came to a halt. Rick showed up at my apartment with the boys and handed them over to me. He said, "Here, Jenny. You can have them." In court that day, too tormented and emotionally drained to speak for myself, the attorney I had been consulting stood up and spoke for me. He explained to the judge that Rick had relinquished his parental rights to the boys. In Rick's absence, the judge granted me sole physical and legal custody, more than I had asked or hoped for. Rick immediately hooked up with someone else. At last, I was free.

———

It had been close to two-and-a half years since I had passed on that full-on kiss from Jonny and ended all contact with him for fear of what Rick would do to me if he found out I was sneaking around. Like we could pick up right where we left off, nervous as ever, I dialed his mom's number. His brother answered.

"Hello?"

"Hi. Is Jonny there?"

"Who? No. He doesn't live here anymore."

"Oh...okay. Thank you."

Hoping he was just being a jerk to Jonny, like older brothers do, and not giving him his messages, I tried again a few days later but received the same response. I couldn't believe it. The last time I'd seen Jonny, he was clean, drug-free. If he didn't live with his parents any longer, he must have met someone else and moved on. It had taken me too long to get out. Shattered, on one hand I felt a great sense of wide-open freedom; on the other, I felt scared.

Living on my own was hard, but I loved my cozy apartment in town. The boys and I swam in the complex's pool and enjoyed the hot tub. Sometimes Lori joined us, too. Like in Concow Lake, if she didn't have a bathing suit, she'd lay low in shorts and a bra. I worked and took care of my boys and continued in counseling. I tried to trust that "If you don't do the hard work of becoming whole on your own, all of your relationships will fall disappointingly flat." Tim said he was going to frame that quote for me. He eventually did.

Maybe I couldn't handle being alone, or maybe I was just a fool. To get close to me, a guy in our apartment complex started spending time with Zack and Tony at the pool. He invited them to pizza. A divorcee with three kids of his own, he didn't do drugs or smoke pot, and seemed to be a family man. I had been free from Rick a mere three months when I became involved with Bert.

Lori's take on him: "Jenny, a small step might seem like a big step compared to Rick."

Aunt Jeannie, whom I remember just prior to the end of her eighteen-year marriage sitting at her kitchen table, wearing large, dark sunglasses to hide her black eyes: "I hope he's a professional."

Tim asked, "What are you going to do when the right person comes along and you're tied up in a relationship?"

Although I knew they were right, I stayed with Bert even when he asked, "You have a thing for him (Tim), don't you?"

"No." But, of course; Tim had been the only person I could count on. Still, I dropped out of counseling and, at the end of my six-month lease, Bert and I moved in together to save money.

While I was caught up in my new relationship, Lori and Seth's marriage was falling apart. Lori complained to me that Seth spent all his time at his mother's, leaving none for her. When he enlisted in the armed services—unbeknownst to his wife—my sister's life took a hard turn. Mom called: "Jenny, Lori's using again."

After all the good years of her being clean, I was devastated. "What?"

Mom answered, "Yes."

I confronted Lori: "Mom says you're using again."

"Yeah. And Mom keeps asking me to get her some."

It was no use.

As for her marriage, Lori said Seth couldn't get beyond her past. She confronted *me*: "Seth said Brooke told him that you were against us getting married in the first place."

In the beginning, I did think they were crazy, but I was adamant that I was never against it. The truth is, in the end, Seth was lucky: he got the best part of my sister.

As the divorce went forward, Brooke and I went our separate ways, taking sides for our respective sibling. Lori returned to what she knew best and where there was nothing, or no one, to lose— except a significant amount of time in prison, if caught with dope again.

Bert and I bought a low-end house with a built-in swimming pool and planned to get married on Valentine's Day of the following year, 1999. I came home from work one day to a message on my answering machine. It was Lori asking, "Jenny, can you call me back, please?" It had been months since I'd heard from her. I feared she was looking for a place to stay, and there was no way I was letting meth into my home. I didn't return her call. Had I known how the year was going to unfold, I would have returned her call a thousand times over. Maybe she just needed a clean place to regroup. Maybe she would have moved in and brought meth and all its troubles. Maybe she wanted someone, a sister, to talk to. I will never know, because on December 6, 1998, life changed.

Bert and I had spent the day playing in the snow above Concow with Mom, Billy Jack, and several of my nieces and nephews. It was an odd day, being with my family, because we rarely did things together anymore, but we had fun. At one point, Bert's and my truck got stuck in snow. While the guys were digging it out, I sat inside watching Mom in hers. It was obvious she had lost a lot of weight. I wondered if that was due to meth, because when Lori was in it, Mom was, too. Although rather distant, my mother would feign a smile, and even a laugh, when spoken to. Repeatedly throughout the day, as well as while sitting in her truck, she used her asthma inhaler. *Puff, puff, hold. Puff, puff, hold.* After digging our vehicle out, it stalled. We called for a tow truck. When it arrived late that evening, Bert and I said our goodbyes to my family and parted ways.

No sooner had Bert and I made it through our front door than Mom and Billy Jack pulled into our driveway. Mom was crying. She had been informed by the police that Lori, while traveling through the Feather River Canyon earlier that day, had died in a car wreck.

The news of Lori's death was shocking. I had never lost anyone before. All I could think about was the last time I had seen her. Cavorting in a white lacy dress, she was embarrassed about getting caught wearing no panties during a physical for a job she had applied for. She laughed and said, "The doctor was cute, though!"

In the days between her death and funeral, I went through some grief stages that are hard to explain. First, I was in disbelief—but her four children were without a mom now, so it was real. Preston went full time with his father, Stephanie and Steven moved back in with Mom and Billy Jack, Sam apparently went *everywhere*. Second, I was of the mindset that, *Well, with the lifestyle that she led, it was bound to happen.*

Family and friends, some I hadn't seen in a long time and some I didn't even know, showed up for her funeral. And, much to my surprise, so did Jonny—with a female companion. A glamour portrait of Lori rested on a tripod next to her closed casket.

Several people stood up and spoke, including sixteen-year-old Sam. I couldn't find the courage to speak. Instead, I played "Angel" by Sarah McLaughlin, a song I first heard on the Tuesday after my sister's death. For those who wanted to gather after the ceremony, I opened my home for a barbecue. When I invited Jonny and his friend, he gave me a "this is awkward" look and said, "I don't know. We'll see." They didn't make it.

You're not supposed to lose your siblings until you're old. I still couldn't believe Lori was really gone; I'd never see her or hear her laughter again. The third stage of grief I went through wasn't really a stage, but a reality check: life is short, really short. Lori's ended at only thirty-three years old; I wanted mine lived with no regrets.

Until Lori's service, it had been five years since I'd seen Jonny. Once again, he looked healthy and clean, drug-free. I was engaged to Bert, but I couldn't get past the fact that Jonny was my destiny. And I was his, not his thin friend with long brown hair, like me—who had signed the funeral guest book with his last name! *He couldn't really be married, right?* Bert was a family man, but Jonny *was* my family. I never understood what happened between us way back when: was it me, or meth? Now that he was clean and I was "out"—well, sort of—I needed to know. On my behalf, Sam confirmed with him that he was, in fact, not married. She also asked him if he was still interested in me.

His answer: "Yes. I've always loved Jennie-fer."

I dropped my fiancé like a bad habit. Amid our sudden separation, I was fine with leaving behind everything we had accumulated, but he chose to take only half. As for the house, I was okay with letting him have that, too, but he opted to move out and eventually signed it over to me. Sam, scrambling to find a home, moved in with me. My new life, lived with no regrets, had arrived.

When Zack and Tony were at their father's house, sometimes things at mine got a little crazy. That New Year's Eve, I decided to throw a party. As family and friends took turns on someone's beer bong, a couple had tied up the bathroom for a long, long time. They had the faucet running, I assume to stifle the sound of whatever they were doing in there. Apparently, they didn't think the music was loud enough. Well, my sink had a slow drain. When they finally opened the door, water had spilled over the basin and flooded the floor. They were embarrassed; I was ticked off, but not for long. After cleaning it up, I rejoined my party. It was so cold that night that the water in the hose was frozen solid, but when the clock struck twelve, the brave girls—me included—polar-beared it into the swimming pool in our birthday suits. Talk about high beams!

The get-togethers at my place weren't always as eventful as that New Year's Eve party; most involved my family and I grieving over Lori's death. We spent many barbecues searching through old pictures and telling the same stories over and over. When we ran out of tears, some of us started asking questions. I wanted to know who had molested Lori at eight. Besides me, only two people in our group—Sam and Lonny's wife Amy—knew about it, but they didn't know who the perpetrator was. I also wanted to know how my mom could have been such a horrible mother. Lori had started using meth at only fourteen. When she was older and wanted to shoot up, Mom was the one to show her how to do it "properly." I couldn't understand. I really wanted to rip her to shreds for her lousy parental choices, but I could tell a part of her had died along with Lori. Mom knew what she had and hadn't done as a mother, and I believed she was truly sorry. Lori, during her sober years, had stated to many people that she forgave Mom for everything; knowing that gave me a tiny sliver of peace.

At one of our gatherings, I learned that Sam, too, had started using meth at only fourteen. When Lori told her to stop, Sam said, "No. Only if you do." Like mother like daughter...Lori passed the torch—and the meth pipe—on to Sam. Disgusted, I was grateful that Sam now was living at my house and clean.

During one of those barbecues, the person I needed most, Jonny, showed up. I was so happy to see him. Like we hadn't missed a beat, in no time I was sitting on his lap and we were sharing kisses again. It felt completely natural. That afternoon, we ate great food, drank beer, and laughed hard. That night, I cried hard. We crashed in my bed, I in my panties and he in his boxers. Just like old times, he held me tight in his arms.

The next day was the same—just catching up. Jonny showed me a picture of his young daughter with whom he was trying to get in touch. I showed him a picture of his young self I hadn't been able to part with. When I told him how crazy I was about him way back when, sounding surprised, he asked, "Why?"

"I loved you, that's why." I left out the part about having a name for our someday daughter, Jonni Dannielle, but filled him in on the plans I'd made for our future: "I wanted to get a job, a car, and then move into a cozy little apartment together." He looked at me like I was insane.

I explained what happened after our last meeting at his place: "I tried to leave Rick, but he wouldn't let me go. I thought he was going to kill me." I couldn't tell whether Jonny understood the gravity of the abuse I'd received from Rick or not. "When I finally did get out and into my own place, I called your parents' house twice, but your brother told me you didn't live there anymore."

"What? I live right across the street. The lady that I used to do yard work for passed away and left me her house. I have my own house."

Timing had never been on our side as far as our relationship was concerned, but Jonny and I were finally together, and that was all that mattered. That night, as we lay in bed together, I wanted to love him, but, for whatever reason, he didn't reciprocate; instead, he just held me. That was enough. He went home the next morning after breakfast. We continued telephone contact.

One crazy day, Jonny went along with my madness in grabbing his nicest shirt and joining me in a photo op to redeem a gift certificate for a canvas portrait, which wouldn't be ready for pickup for several weeks. After the shoot, I drove us to my house. Once there, he asked to borrow my car; he didn't own one. I said yes. Several hours went by with no word from him. I dialed his number, but there was no answer. The only person I knew to check with was Uncle Henry, Billy Jack's brother who had years earlier brought Jonny down to help us move from Stockton. Uncle Henry didn't know where he was either, but said, "I told him, 'Jonny, if you're going to be with Jenny, you can't be doing that *stuff* anymore.'" I'd thought he *wasn't* doing "that stuff" anymore.

When Jonny finally phoned me, he said his "friend," the female one who'd accompanied him to Lori's funeral, had a sister who had just gotten busted for a meth lab. He explained that he'd been running around trying to find out what was going on with that. When he brought my car back, still wearing his nicest shirt, I was far from happy when I dropped him at his house.

Several days passed, and I hadn't heard from Jonny, so Sam took it upon herself to find out why. When she called, she heard his female friend in the background asking, "Who's that? Who are you talking to?" When Jonny and I spoke next, he said the girl sensed "something was up" and asked him, "What's going on?" *I was wondering that, too!* He told me he couldn't "just do this to her like that." *Do what to her like that?* I gave him space and continued to wait it out, until I couldn't wait any longer.

"Hello?" Short of breath and talking quietly, he answered the phone as if I'd caught him at a bad (in the middle of sex) time.

"Hi. What are you doing?"

"I'll have to call you back."

"When?"

"I don't know..."

I couldn't believe it. *Was it me, or meth?* Apparently, it was both.

When the canvas portrait of Jonny and me arrived, it looked nothing like the way I'd imagined our life together. I tore it up into as many pieces as my bare hands could and threw it into the outside trash can. In that moment, I took my greatest stand: I was not going to be second—to anything or anyone—ever again. A few weeks later, there was a knock at my door. To my surprise, it was Jonny with a bouquet of red roses. I accepted the flowers and softly said, "Thank you." With his ride waiting in the drive-way and no other words spoken between us, I didn't know what Jonny was trying to say to me that day, but when he turned to leave, I closed the door.

———

Questions I had about Lori's life and death lingered in the back of my mind. When I learned that family members could order the coroner's autopsy report on her body, I requested it. In part, it read:

> *The body is that of a normally developed, well-nourished white female appearing older than her recorded age of 33 years, weighing 139 pounds and measuring 5 feet 7 inches in height.*
>
> *On the back is a dark-colored tattoo of a butterfly. Over the midline of the back is an additional dark-colored tattoo of the words "Ladies Love Outlaws." On the volar (palm side) aspect of the left lower arm is a green and red indecipherable tattoo (a rose).*
>
> *In the right antecubital fossa (tiny triangular depression on the front of the elbow) is an area of purple-red contusion measuring $1\frac{1}{2} \times 1$ inches. Central to this contusion is a pinpoint red-brown apparent abrasion. Overall, this has the appearance of a needle track. In addition, there are several irregular to round scars present in the right antecubital fossa.*
>
> *Comprehensive Blood Screen: Ethanol = 0.19 GM%*
>
> *Methamphetamine = 373 ng/ml*
>
> *Amphetamine = 138 ng/ml*

Lori was really gone. With Stevie Nicks' "Talk to Me" drowning out the noise of the tragedy, the horrific scene played over and over in my mind: Lori, driving with a car full of people, drops her son Preston off at Seth's. She stops at someone's house to shoot up, then leaves for Nevada. There's a look on her face of hopelessness, like even the old way of escaping no longer suffices. On her way back to California, having consumed alcohol, she's driving too fast through the Feather River Canyon. Hitting black ice, she loses control of the car and slams into the granite wall. Lori dies, but the three passengers survive.

I was faced with the realization that, just like I'd lost Lori, given their lifestyle I could lose all my close family members to an untimely death. There was nothing I could do about it. I became angry—and felt slighted. Maybe I was a mistake by God's standards; therefore, sentenced to a lifetime of calamities. Spinning out of control, I called Tim to return to therapy. He'd said it before, and he said it again: "Jenny, you need to stop feeling sorry for yourself." He reminded me, "If you don't do the hard work of becoming whole on your own, all of your relationships will fall disappointingly flat." And, most important, "You teach people how to treat you by what you tolerate." I understood all that. Then he said I didn't respect men, and that left me confused. I thought I loved men, men just didn't love me.

I was single, and not by choice. Lonny's wife Amy and I, having our love for Lori in common, started hanging out. For fun, the two of us enrolled in country-western line dance classes at the recreation center. We were there every Thursday night and we'd practice at our barbecues on the weekends. When we learned a few dances well enough, we accompanied the rest of our class to the Crazy Horse Saloon on Wednesday evenings from six to nine for even more lessons. We'd dance the entire time minus the couples' dances. When those happened, I longed to be asked out onto the floor, yet in those months among cowboys, I was asked only once—by the line dance instructor. He had to have felt sorry for me. Nevertheless, I loved Amy and my Wednesday nights cutting it up on the western scene and, in time, I owned a nice pair of Ariats for dancing and a cute little white Jeep Wrangler 4x4 for driving.

In addition to line dancing at the Crazy Horse Saloon, Amy and I were soon taking ballroom dance lessons at Molly Gunn's on Saturdays. There I was finally asked to dance by someone other than the instructor. It was once and by a military veteran. After we did the Cha-Cha to Santana's "Smooth," the man lifted his pantleg, showed me his prosthetic limb, and said, "I bet you wouldn't have believed I could dance like that!" He was right. Amy, although pregnant, was asked to dance several times at Molly Gunn's. Once, she sat at the table with her water with lemon, she didn't drink alcohol while expecting, when she was invited out onto the floor.

"No, thank you. I'm pregnant."

The guy responded, "No way. Now I've heard everything."

She stood up from the table to prove it. He walked off with an alarming look on his face.

Most nights when we went out, Amy, the designated driver, drove us in my Jeep. Stuck on the Dixie Chicks' *Wide Open Spaces* and *Fly* CDs, "Goodbye Earl" was our ride-home song. That is, until I attempted to pop it into the CD player late one night and the wind caught it just right. The CD flew out onto Highway 70, never to be heard again.

That year, Amy and I floated across the dance floors doing the West Coast Swing, Foxtrot, and the Cha-Cha, to name a few; and we line-danced to "Cherokee Fiddle," "Watermelon Crawl," "All Shook Up," and all the other songs we knew the choreography to. I rode a mechanical bull, and even came close to head-banging in a mosh pit. Through all the fun, not once did someone try to pick me up. It was weird.

It wasn't until December, about a year after losing Lori, that someone showed interest in me. It was a past acquaintance. Like Rick, he was a bit older than me—I'd been there, done that. I declined his invitation to a Y2K New Year's Eve party, opting to watch the ball drop in Times Square on television at home with my boys. I doubted that the world was really going to end, but I wasn't entirely sure. That acquaintance was persistent, though, and I eventually caved in to keeping "good company," as he'd say; however, I kept one foot in the stirrup, so to speak. When we did things together, I either covered my half or picked up the full tab the next time. I'd owe no one anything.

Also at about the year mark after losing Lori, I got a call from Dad. He was happy to tell me that he had heard from Penny. Excitedly, he said, "You won't believe what business she's in!"

"What?"

"The movie business; in production!"

"Really? Wow!" I *couldn't* believe it.

Dad must have told Penny about me, too, because she soon called and we got to chat for the first time. She had had no idea about me. That prompted a call to Debbie from one of us, I'm not sure who now. This time, Debbie was a little more receptive. Penny arranged for a visit with Dad that I joined, but Debbie couldn't make it. Of all my family members, Penny was the only one who looked like me. It was totally cool to see someone I was related to that had the same problem finding sunglasses: our noses just don't want to be positioned right. But the best thing was seeing somebody that I was connected to turn out healthy, successful, and, most of all, drug-free. I wasn't the only one anymore. Penny was like a portal, someone for me to look up to that had made it; proof that "making it" really is possible.

Penny was about to move to the United Kingdom for six months to a year to work on the upcoming *Harry Potter and the Sorcerer's Stone* movie. Before she left, she, her husband Stewart, Zack, Tony, my older "friend," and I went for an overnight trip to Fort Bragg, California. We visited Glass Beach and even ventured out whale watching. At the end of our trip, Penny gave me a glass vial full of colorful beach glass with a heart-shaped red one glued to the front. That was accompanied by a 4-by-6 index card with a cut-out picture of us by the ocean with the Cabrillo Lighthouse in the background. She labeled the card "Hearts." Sometime later she sent me the book *A Girl's Guide to Hunting and Fishing*. She must have sensed something was off with my man-hunting skills.

My "good company" relationship phased out. Since I could take care of myself, I was determined not to live with or become committed to anyone until I was sure that it was the right person. I wanted to find someone I could love again and trust with my heart. I wanted to find someone who would love me back. I had no idea if that would ever happen.

CHAPTER NINE

THAT LITTLE WHITE SPECK

As I sat on Tim's sofa, waiting to be called in for my next session, he walked in and slammed a "NO SMOKING" sign on the windowsill...

As I crested the hill, I passed a man in an old, rugged FJ40 Land Cruiser. With a blank stare, as if lost in space, he didn't even check out the chick in the Jeep, but I noticed him. Exactly one week later, Sam and I pulled into the parking lot of a grocery store. I went in to get a gallon of milk. While standing in the checkout line, I noticed a guy come through the front glass double doors. He was pleasingly dressed in western wear—jeans and heavy boots. I thought nothing of it. After paying, with milk in hand, I exited the store. Back at my Jeep, Sam was laughing hysterically. She must have had her fill of me whining *"I'm going to be alone at ninety,"* because she asked,

"Aunt Jenny, did you see a good-looking guy in there?"

"Actually, I did. Why?"

Sam laughed her boisterous, distinct laugh. "Because I left your phone number in his Jeep thing!"

"What?"

"Yes! He pulled in here with his music blaring. I was like, *oh yeah!*"

I thought she was crazy. We both laughed some more as I drove off.

Later that night, the phone rang and Sam answered. After a brief chat with the person on the line, grinning ear to ear, she exclaimed, "Aunt Jenny, someone found a note that said to call you!" and passed me the phone.

I grabbed the receiver from her. "Hello?"

"Hi, my name's Scott. Someone wrote your number on a napkin with a note to call Jenny and left it in my Land Cruiser."

"Oh, my God! My niece did that. I am so sorry."

"No, it's all right," he said. "I actually crumpled up the napkin and threw it in the trash. After a while, I was bored and thought, well, maybe I'll see who it is."

We talked for more than two hours that night. Right before hanging up, he said, "You can call me back tomorrow if you want, but you don't have to."

I really liked the "but you don't have to" part, so I called the following evening. We spoke for two to three hours each night for a solid week, then we met in person. When his FJ40 Land Cruiser pulled into my driveway, I realized I'd been talking to the same man I'd seen two weeks earlier. *Crazy!* At my front door, while his boys were at baseball practice, wearing a light green T-shirt, Wranglers, heavy-duty boots, and a forward-facing baseball cap with a Promise Keepers pin in it, his smile was warm and eyes soft blue. He reached out with a firm but tender handshake and a "Hello, my name's Matt." Chuckling, he added, "Scott's my middle name." After a brief conversation, he turned to get back to his boys' practice. When he was out of my driveway, I hit the "random play" button on my CD changer, then fell onto the couch. Stevie Nicks' "Leather and Lace" came on—perfect!

Through ongoing talks with Matt, I learned that he was the black sheep in a strong Christian family who believed in living by the rules, and then some. Attend church regularly, no premarital sex, divorce, or taking part in anything that wasn't "of God"— which, being born out of wedlock, had been my entire existence. The second to the youngest of five, Matt had been born with the umbilical cord wrapped around his neck and almost didn't make it into the world. "I could barely move during my entire first year, I'm told, but after that, there was no stopping me!" He laughed. Unlike my many homes, he said he'd grown up in the same house from the time he was four. And, opposite to mine, he described his family as being hard workers. "There's no such thing as a free lunch," he quoted his father. For the most part, according to Matt, the men in his family were wage earners and the women homemakers, especially if they had young children. He mentioned his mom and matriarch, Millie, kept a close eye on her clan, including the adults, also different from mine, but he seemed to have a good relationship with her, and I felt that was a great sign.

Matt was on the tail end of a thirteen-year marriage that had created three very amazing young men: Matt, twelve; Tom, ten; and Taylor, eight. I listened heartfully when he talked of the things he was doing to reconcile his family, which was his hope, like receiving pastoral counseling, but it just wasn't happening for him. When the time was right, he told Millie, his mother, about me: "Her name's Jennifer. She's made almost every mistake in the book." That didn't do me any favors. At least he added, "She had a tough upbringing, but made something of herself." Our first family dinner together was quite awkward.

After meeting his clan, Matt and I spent many days together either at his house or mine. We barbecued and the boys swam. We watched movies over and over together. In *Urban Cowboy*, every time Bud placed Sissy's name plate back in his rear window, I cried. During *Pure Country*, every time Ernest Tucker explained, "The funny thing about that little white speck on the top of chicken shit, that little white speck is chicken shit, too," I reflected on my past and cried again. One evening, Matt said right before we met he'd prayed for his next partner to be someone who hadn't been born with a silver spoon in her mouth yet had chosen to make something of herself. Embarrassed, I giggled, "You might want to be careful what you wish for."

The new additions to my life—Matt and *two* sisters—had me on cloud nine. To top it off, when Penny was settled in the U.K. for her work, she said if we could get there, Zack, Tony, and I could stay with her at her flat in London. I jumped at the opportunity for my boys and me to see some of Europe. Luckily, Dad offered to pay for the pricy plane tickets. After passports and a fourteen-hour flight, we all landed at London's Heathrow Airport.

Penny had to work but created a jam-packed itinerary for our seven-day trip that included going to Rome. We visited Buckingham Palace, Westminster Abbey, The Tower of London, The Houses of Parliament and Big Ben, the River Thames, and Madame Tussaud's Wax Museum. I shared a belated birthday celebration with Penny's husband, Stewart, at London's Hard Rock Cafe. During our adventure, an Englishman standing next to us on a bus brashly stated, "Bloody Americans. They think there's only one way to do things." Loving his accent, I shrugged his comment off. Through her work connections, Penny arranged a tour of the set for the *Harry Potter and the Sorcerer's Stone* movie she was working on. Stewart took us aboard the train to Leavesden Studios. The "stone" walls of the Great Hall that were plaster were fascinating, but I loved the very real-looking goblin mask molds. I learned the set designers had to stick every single hair into the unicorn's body—all the intricate details were mind-boggling. With everybody doing their small part, it was such collaboration to create something so amazing.

From London, my boys and I flew to Rome. Precisely following Penny's handwritten sight-seeing map, we walked for hours. We visited the Colosseum, the Pantheon, climbed the Spanish Steps, and made a wish in the Trevi Fountain. We walked through St. Peter's Basilica but had to skip the Vatican because of the long line. Unaware of mad-cow disease in Europe, I enjoyed a steak dinner and the boys had a burger. When I asked, "Where's the butter?" for my bread, I got a nasty look from the waiter—

they dip their bread in olive oil instead. After two nights (covered by Penny) in Rome, we flew back to London, said our goodbyes, and caught our flight home.

Back in Oroville, Matt and I had been seeing each other for more than six months when he received word from his wife that she was going to move out of state. Their boys—Matt, Tom, and Taylor—were to stay with him. The day she left, Matt cried in my arms. Much later he said he was upset only because of the loss his sons suffered in being separated from their mother, but I knew better. Within three weeks of her move, he received her call that she wanted to come back to California. Feeling out of place, I watched Matt and his boys light up at the news of her return. That light lessened as the weeks turned into months with no steps forward on her part. Then she asked to move onto the back porch of what had once been their home, but, unsure of her intentions, Matt said no. By then, he was done.

As if Matt wasn't going through enough at the time, his landlord gave notice that he wanted to retire in his rental, so now Matt had to move. I was certain about my feelings for him, I loved Matt, plus we were together every day anyway, so I offered up my home for him and his three boys. After much thought, he accepted. Once he and his boys were settled in, the fact that we were cohabitating—living in sin—brought about questions of our future, as in marriage, from his family. Their prodding irked Matt, but not me; I had every intention of marrying him. Six months after his wife had left the state, she made it back to town. Matt started divorce proceedings, which ended by way of an amicable settlement.

As Matt's and my relationship moved forward, I began a perplexing one with Millie. During one of our conversations, she told me, "I get whatever I pray for—if I ask God for sunshine, I get it—except when it comes to people's actions." That seemed a bit odd, but I knew how she felt about divorce, and her son had just gone through one. I figured that was what she was talking about. In another conversation, she shared that she'd always carried a deep fear that someone would take Matt from her. Knowing she'd almost lost him at his birth, that made sense to me, too. But then, nearly shedding tears, she said, "I can't believe you love my son." Now that I didn't understand. To add to my confusion, per Matt, I learned that after that chat she'd privately warned him: "She's not going to take any shit." Later, he said he interpreted her statement to mean that I wasn't going to take any of *his* shit, and it never crossed his mind that she meant that I wasn't going to take any of *her* shit.

Instead of ending counseling with Tim—like I'd done when I met Bert—Matt was interested and willing to learn healthy tools for our relationship, so I started it up again, this time with him. The three of us unpacked the baggage Matt and I carried from our pasts, which was a lot, so it wouldn't interfere with our future together. We spent a great deal of time mediating boundaries. For example, Matt changed every station on my car's stereo to Christian music—*nobody messes with my music*. After I got over being irritated, I realized that I liked Christian music, too, so I left one station alone. Another example was that I didn't have to coddle Matt all the time, even though he liked it.

In Matt, I found a loyal companion; a man I loved and felt

would never abandon me. He was someone I could tell all my secrets to, and it was okay. As I entrusted him with details of my many struggles, he offhandedly said, "You remind me of a cockroach—you could live through anything!"

Reveling in his comment, I laughed out loud as I told him about Mom's story titled "Corky the Cockroach." Then I added, "Corky has many battle wounds and scars."

Matt likened my childbearing "scars" to fiddle-back, the beautiful wood grain of a fine rifle which makes it so exclusive.

I knew I had found my partner, and with Matt not yet taking the initiative, over dinner on Valentine's Day of 2001, I asked him to marry me. He chuckled like I'd stolen his thunder, but he accepted. We planned to marry the following year.

Mom and Billy Jack had spent a decade and a half in Concow before deciding to move back to Oroville. They had rented a house initially, but now were buying one, albeit from a loan shark. Lori's death had taught me how quickly life can change, so now that Mom lived in town, I tried to see her often. She wasn't getting any younger, or healthier for that matter, and the thought of losing her too terrified me. One day, I took her to the pharmacy to pick up her medications. For the entire trip, hunched over in the passenger's seat of my car, she held a towel over a small cut on her leg. Every time she'd remove the towel, blood flowed down her leg. She said it was because she was taking blood thinners. The next thing I knew, on my way to meet Matt for one of our counseling sessions, I received a call that she'd had an intracerebral hemorrhage, a stroke. I could barely get the words out to Tim when I called to cancel my appointment. Thankfully, after a short stay in the ICU, Mom recovered. She was left, however, with severe headaches that called for potent opioid pain medication. Although busy with all the new people in my life, I kept an eye on her.

Sam had left my home at age eighteen and moved in with her boyfriend. When that relationship failed, she, like her mother Lori had done, turned to meth. I'd had no idea where she was living until my upset mom called: "Jenny, Jonny kicked Sam out and threw all her clothes into the street. Can you go over there, please?" The last thing I needed was to meet up with Jonny again; that never turned out well. Besides, Mom and Billy Jack lived right around the corner from him in Southside; I felt Billy Jack could handle it.

"Mom, I can't. I'm sorry."

It was months before I'd heard anything more of Sam. When I did, it was directly from her by way of a phone call: "Aunt Jenny, I met someone! His name is Kevin, and he is a good man. I am so happy! We met within our circle of...you know, connections... but while destitute and sleeping in our car, one day we decided we didn't want to live that way anymore. We're on our way to Tennessee, where he has a job waiting for him!" After thanking God that she was clean again, I thanked her for leaving that note with my number in Matt's rig. I told her we were getting married. With that boisterous, distinct laugh of hers, she exclaimed, "Look! I blessed you, and God blessed me!" Life was good.

My people were doing well, and my job was about to get a whole lot better. Through the deposition firm I worked for, I learned of an official court reporter position about to open at the

Butte County Superior Court, which was right around the corner from Matt's and my home. Landing a job like that meant I'd no longer be self-employed, the pay was twice what I was earning, the benefits were exceptional, and I wouldn't have the thirty-minute commute to and from Chico, where most of the depositions took place, anymore. It was a great step up for our family. The only downside was I'd be working with judges and "young attorneys in Bimmers," as Rick used to criticize, but I didn't think of that until I noticed Matt's uneasiness about the move. When I told my soon-to-be mother-in-law, Millie, about it, I didn't receive the reaction I was expecting from her either. Had I been hoping for fireworks and a party? I didn't feel like my support system was there. This step up was huge for me. I went for it anyway.

When the opening posted, I applied for the job. With seven years of deposition experience under my belt, I felt the position had come at the perfect time, thus it was meant to be mine. However, as they say, "If you fail to prepare, you prepare to fail." I did very little studying because I thought that I'd learn the details of the job *after* I was hired. On the day of the interview, I was so nervous I froze up in front of the panel of four professionals. Not knowing most of the answers to the specific official court reporter questions, or even the general ones, my best answer was, "I would ask my supervisor." I left in tears, crying about how badly I had blown it. I told myself I would never set foot in that courthouse again.

Matt felt my pain that evening and was there to console me as I sat in my bed, still in my interview suit, with my arms wrapped around my pillow bawling like a baby. In the next days, sensing some sort of relief in Millie and maybe even Matt about my failure, I figured they were just afraid of change; eventually they would trust my intentions. The letter arrived in the mail a week or so later thanking me for my interest but regretting to inform me that I had not gotten the job. My work and life would still be the same, which was okay, but I had *really* wanted that position.

At the start of the new year, 2002, I was ready to plan Matt's and my wedding. Standing in the grocery store line, I picked up my first bridal magazine to take home, look through, and get some idea of what I wanted in a dress. Browsing through it later that evening, the pullout was the back of a beautiful satin, ivory, A-line, strapless dress. There were tiny, delicate metallic leaf designs scattered beautifully over the fabric. It had soft buttons down to the waist where there were three tightly-wrapped satin roses for the bustle. Immediately below, the dress split and gradually separated, a tulle court train underneath. As I read down the page, it said, "Cover, February 2002, *Modern Bride Magazine*." I looked again at the cover, and there was the front of the dress in the pullout. It had a sweetheart neckline and a beautiful matching lacy bolero.

As soon as I could, I took the magazine to the bridal shop in the next town. I asked the manager, "Do you have something like this?"

She said, "That's Alfred Angelo. I have *that* dress."

I couldn't wait to see it and try it on. Aside from a few needed alterations, it fit me perfectly. I knew I had found my dress;

plus, it was on sale for a price that even persuaded Dad to offer to pay for it. I accepted.

To keep Mom in the loop about my wedding plans, I stopped by her house one afternoon to show her my dress—on the cover of the magazine. Aside from her nose being completely bandaged from undergoing surgery for a deviated septum, she looked great. We visited for a short time, then I gave her a hug goodbye. I was walking toward my car when I heard her, with a baffled voice, call my name, "Jenny?"

I turned around and answered, "Yes?"

Sounding as if she was speaking through her nose, she said, "It's my birthday."

I couldn't believe I had forgotten. Feeling like a heel, I walked over and gave her another hug and told her happy birthday. I left but showed up later with some cute kitchen hand towels and a card.

A fan of Richard Simmons, Mom used to sit in our Concow living room and enjoy watching him get his group revved up—the more she toked on a joint, the more she enjoyed the show—but not once had I ever seen her "get off the couch," like he urged. As my "big day" approached, I began to see a spark in Mom I'd never seen before. She started eating healthier meals, like switching out ground beef for ground turkey and fried chicken for baked "chicken tits," as she'd call it. I caught her drinking leftover juice from canned spinach and walked in on her doing Tae Bo with Billy Blanks. I was dumbfounded by what could be fueling her spark until, putting two and two together, I realized my dad would be at my wedding. Mom hadn't seen her old flame since we'd run into him at the store when I was two. Even if only temporary, it was wonderful to see her lit up.

For my bridal shower, thrown by my soon-to-be in-laws, Mom stepped out of her comfort zone, looking amazing in some new but casual clothing, and attended. She was the only one from my family that showed up, and I was proud of her for that. I thought things went well at the event, but over the course of the afternoon, the conversation among the gathering of women, aside from my mom, included terms like "poor" man's glue, "poor" man's spackle, and even "poor" white trash. "Raised by wolves" was also thrown into the mix. Mom sat there quietly. The gathering ended with a nice hug between Millie and my mom, and many lovely gifts for Matt and me. Mom later told me that she felt the uncouth comments at my shower had been directed at her. I thought she was being overly sensitive...that is, until a few days before the wedding, when my soon-to-be sister-in-law Leah called and asked Mom if she wanted to go shopping in her closet for something to wear. Then I knew something was up. Mom said she politely declined, "No, thank you. I already have something."

With the wedding just around the corner, Millie pulled me aside and asked, "Are you absolutely sure that you want to get married?"

"Yes," I answered without hesitation.

"Because, as I have told every one of my kids and their partners," she explained, "you can change your mind up to the very last second, even the day of, but after you're married, there's no backing out."

I was sure I wanted to marry Matt.

The northern California forecast in late May can be unpredictable, so I prayed with Millie for my outdoor nuptial to be blessed with beautiful weather. Thankfully, she got what we both wanted; the morning of, at Clotilde Merlo Park in Stirling City, California, it was gorgeous and sunny.

More than a hundred fifty people, not counting children, had been invited to attend Matt's and my wedding. From where I waited in hiding with Dad, given all the chatter, it sounded like most had made it. Once the music started, everyone quieted down; Dad and I listened carefully for our cue to commence down the wooden walkway. Right on time, we stepped from our secreted trail and into the entry of the outdoor chapel. On the far side was a large wooden cross attached to a tall pine tree. Below that stood our pastor. Matt, wearing Wranglers, a long-sleeve ivory shirt with a dark brown leather vest, and his White's Smokejumper boots, was positioned next to his groomsmen, our five boys. Opposite them was my one bridesmaid, Amy. As Dad and I proceeded down the aisle, we passed Matt's family in the pews on one side and my family on the other. Seated between Billy Jack and Grandma Maggie, Mom looked beautiful in her green and purple floral outfit that matched perfectly the wildflower theme of the occasion. Debbie and her husband Jerry were there, too. At the end of our walk, Dad gave me away and then took his seat next to Pat.

The ceremony began with a prayer from the pastor, followed by Matt and me sharing communion. During the recitation of our vows, we exchanged rings. Matt's was an indestructible titanium band; mine an heirloom from Penny that I had personalized with seven diamonds, one for each member of my blended family, plus an eighth one for God. Seven, the number symbolic of completion, and eight, the number symbolic of new beginnings, represented exactly where I was in life. At the same time, those numbers meant closure to a past I'd wanted to forget. Matt and I shared our first kiss as husband and wife, then our first dance to George Strait's "I Cross My Heart" at the reception. That was the most amazing day, and I left it convinced that God loves even this "little white speck."

As soon as the high from our wedding wore off, I had my dress cleaned and preserved in an air-tight box; I changed my last name—my maiden name wasn't my real name anyway; and I sorted through the many beautiful photographs of the day, picking out my favorite to be enlarged and professionally framed. Starting fresh, after repainting, I redecorated our living room in new furniture and window coverings. As I carefully centered our finished wedding portrait on our wall, I was amazed that I had managed to land a loving, loyal, and handsome husband. I never thought that would happen. I treasured that I was a wife to Matt and a mom and stepmom to our boys. My heart was full.

———

Debbie and Jerry had made it to my wedding despite being smack-dab in the middle of building their custom home, and that meant a lot to me. In the days that followed, my sister looked to be "in a better place" regarding the shock of meeting her long-lost sibling, me, so when we were invited, Matt and I took a jaunt down to Pioneer, California, where Debbie and Jerry lived.

Unlike Penny and me, Debbie and I looked nothing alike. Our similarities were harder to find, but they were there. Right away I could tell we were both quiet, reserved, people-watchers, but it wasn't until my visit after she and Jerry had finished and moved into their custom-built home that I saw our sisterhood ran deep. Debbie had painted the interior sage green, the same color I had recently painted the inside of my home; she had the exact brand leather Lane couch as mine, just a different color; and she even had the exact living room curtains with the macramé top and ends as mine, just a shade darker. We had our style in common, and that was beyond cool.

During that same visit, Debbie pulled out her shoebox of photographs and newspaper clippings, something else we had in common. She showed me an article that confirmed the horrible DUI wreck Dad and his siblings had been in with our drunk grandmother that landed him first in the hospital and then with his brother and sister in foster care. *No wonder Dad had such a horrible track record with women—his own mother nearly killed him!*

Delving into the past together, Debbie could recall only one vague memory of me. She said she'd gone with Dad for a visit to see me when I was a small child, but she wasn't supposed to let out that he was my father. She was unsure why, possibly because there was another man in the picture. We left the conversation, shaking our heads.

———

Until my trip to England, I'd had no idea what *Harry Potter* was, only that Penny said it was going to be big. She was right, and I was beaming with pride over her—my sister's!—success. Matt's family, now officially my in-laws, didn't feel the same, however. They believed *Harry Potter* promoted witchcraft and was "going after the kids." No way. I can't say I didn't see it coming—the year Matt and I became engaged, Millie did away with Easter eggs because they had originated with the pagans. The year we married, she changed "Halloween" to "Reformation Day" and decided against having Christmas trees at Christmastime—Santa had been banished long before I came into the picture. As my mom would say, "To each his own"; I felt Matt and I could do our own thing and live our life as we saw fit. After all, I loved *Harry Potter*, Easter eggs, Halloween, Christmas trees, and Santa Claus.

When *Harry Potter* finally made it to the big screen, religious people picketed our local theater proclaiming the movie's "occult" nature. It opened the day after Millie's birthday. She strongly disapproved of its showing as well, but seated across the kitchen table from her one day, I adamantly said, "I'm going to see it." People typically weren't direct with her like that. Her nose started to bleed. As she tried to stop the flow, she said, "I'm prone to nosebleeds." In hopes of relieving her anxiety about it, I invited her to join Matt and me. She accepted. At the theater, she sat in the seat behind us and prayed through the entire show. Flabbergasted, I wondered what she would have thought about me seeing *The Exorcist* when I was five!

Matt and I had spent two years as a couple before our marriage, but unbeknownst to me, when it came to his family, "to each his own" didn't apply. The more I tried to live my life as I saw fit—celebrating my sister's success with *Harry Potter* and enjoying my holiday preferences—the more bad vibes, glares, and negative comments I received, especially from Millie. I began to question myself. *Am I just being overly sensitive? Is this all in my head? Is this real?*

I realized I wasn't imagining things one day when Matt and I were watching our boys play football. Millie, seated just above us on the bleachers, announced to me, "You know what? As I was getting out of the shower this morning, I had the *worst* thought... don't get pregnant." Matt paid no attention to her comment, but my sister-in-law Leah, who was seated next to her, giggled.

What? I shook it off. I couldn't believe she would say such a thing, since it was none of her business. I had no intention of adding another child to our five, but that was a choice for Matt and me to make as a couple. Her comment put me in tears right there on the spot. She blamed my emotional upset on my beverage—maybe it contained too much sugar? (It was low-calorie.)

The insults kept flying. Leah, as if insinuating that I hadn't made something of myself legitimately, smoothly commented, "It's not where you get, but how you get there." *Well, that can cut both ways.*

For a family dinner, I contributed my signature potato salad. Everyone enjoyed it, even Millie, because after taking a bite, she broadcasted to everyone in the room: "Yum...Jenn trained herself!" I didn't know what to think about that comment. Dogs are trained, not people. Not to mention, those three words, "Jenn trained herself," said a lot about my mother and my upbringing. I began to feel like a stray puppy they had rescued and were coaching to ensure I would never bring them any grief.

Millie took pictures of everyone at a gathering and made a point—several times—to assure me, "I got one of you, too." A few days later, she placed the printed pictures inside a card and dropped it off with Matt at work. When he got home, I opened it to find a picture of everyone but me. I questioned her motives. Was she trying to make me feel less important than the rest of the family? Invisible and disposable? It worked.

I'd gotten my hair highlighted in shades of blond, brown, and deep red, and was seated across from Millie in her kitchen. Other family members were standing around. She said, oh so sweetly, "Jenn, your hair looks so pretty shining there in the flicker of the candlelight."

"Really? Thank you." I appreciated her comment because I knew how hard it was for her to be nice to me.

As Matt and I were leaving, Millie caught me alone on her front porch and carefully took a lock of my hair between her fingers. With a disparaging smile and shake of her head, she softly whispered, "I'm sorry," as if my hair, in truth, was ugly. She then turned around and marched inside; I stepped off the porch and headed home.

Millie gave me a calendar on which she had written each family member's birthday. When my special day came around, she "confused" it with Matt's brother's wife's, Sally, also her daughter-in-law, whom she once described as "a spoiled-rotten little princess" during a rant that I walked in on. My in-laws often "confused" my voice with Sally's, too, when I'd call them on the phone.

During each female roundtable conversation, little barbs were always aimed at me: "Jenn, I love your blouse—it reminds me of a peasant's." That one came from sister-in-law Rebecca, who wasn't quite as adept as the others when it came to slinging insults.

I couldn't believe how I was being treated. I felt like I was back in grammar school on the monkey bars, being tag-teamed by mean girls saying I wasn't wearing any underwear. I weighed everything. *Was this some sort of marriage boot camp they were putting me through, or was I being bullied?*

I talked to Tim about it, and he was brutally honest: "You'd have a hard time coming into my family, too." With a twisted expression on his face, like he couldn't quite believe the things my in-laws were saying and doing to me either, he explained that the reason I couldn't understand why they were so protective of Matt was because I had never *really* been loved. Well, I *really* loved Matt, too, and he wasn't the perpetrator, so divorcing him wasn't a possibility.

My talk with Tim didn't help; I grew apprehensive whenever I had to be around my mother- and sisters-in-law, and *everything* became an attack. I began to feel prayed over to step down from the independence I had worked so hard to gain. Overpowered, I felt trapped, back at war with—a shadow of—Rick. The hardest hit to my freedom would be to take away my livelihood. My greatest fear: Carpal Tunnel Syndrome. I started having a numbing sensation like rubber bands around both of my forearms. CTS would put me out of commission. Stranded. Helpless. Dependent. I continued to work, but I noticed my speech growing rapid at times accompanied by anxiety pains in my chest. That escalated to panic attacks in the restroom at the office. I wasn't sleeping well, and leery about who I could truly trust, I started placing weapons—like a lucky horseshoe and a hammer—near my side of the bed just in case something went awry with Matt. The next thing I knew, I was hiding in my closet from those who might want to harm me. From there, I found myself locked in my bathroom recalling a repressed memory: When I was about three years old, I had awakened in a smoke-filled room, unable to breathe. Through the smoke was a distant doorway. Fearful, alone, and overcome with powerlessness, I screamed for my mom and tried to walk toward the door in search of her. I don't know if I found her or not.

I contacted Tim for an emergency meeting. During the session, staring deep into my eyes as I lost my composure in my sickness, he shook his head and said, "All of my hard work is being undone."

I told him about hiding in my bathroom and recalling myself, at a young age, screaming for my mom in a smoke-filled room. In tears, I mumbled, "What's wrong with me?"

He grumbled to himself, "Is it live, or is it Memorex?" then gently explained that I was experiencing some post-traumatic stress symptoms. I'd had no idea.

As I sat on Tim's sofa, waiting to be called in for my next session, he walked in and slammed a "NO SMOKING" sign on the windowsill across from me. Our next many meetings were spent working on desensitization, a behavioral modification technique used to diminish emotional responsiveness to negative stimuli, or "triggers." During one of the sessions, I spoke of my dog that had gotten hit by a car and died the day before. Oddly enough, Tim said he had spent the night before with Auriga, his German Shepherd, who had died, too. I didn't believe it when he said his dog was gone; I thought he was trying to desensitize me about (my fear of) death, one of my triggers. When I later noticed Auriga's urn on Tim's oak shelf, I learned it was eerily true and had nothing to do with therapy. Several days later, Millie gave me a picture of my dog that she'd taken at an earlier time. She acted sad for my loss.

To regroup, I had to avoid conflict, which meant stepping away from my in-laws. They took it as an insult. Matt, stuck in the middle of it all, was aware that in his past marriage there had been difficulties between his family and wife, but he didn't understand why his family and I were having problems. According to him, "She [his ex-wife] brought a lot of it upon herself." Preparing for the worst, another divorce, Matt shielded his heart and shut me out.

Left to fend for myself, the next time Mom called and asked to borrow money from me, I tore into her: "Why do you only call when you need something? How come we can't do normal mother-daughter things, like go to lunch or visit with each other over coffee? And *why did you expose me to pot as a child?*"

Caught completely off guard, she cried, "Jenny, I'm sorry. You know I'm not social like that. That's just not me. I needed the twenty to pick up my medicine, but I'll figure something else out."

Feeling like I had a legitimate complaint but had acted like an ass, I said, "No, I'm home and I've got it. I'm sorry, too, but I just don't understand."

"That's all right. You're not the only one who feels like we failed as parents."

Billy Jack waited in the car as Mom walked up to my front door. Disgruntled because he never, ever even tried to support her, I handed her the twenty-dollar bill.

I saw a neurologist to deal with the Carpal Tunnel Syndrome. After performing nerve conduction tests, he confirmed that I didn't have it. Instead, I was so stressed-out that my neck muscles were tensing up and pinching the nerves that run down through my arms, which, in turn, was creating the numbing rubber band sensations. He said that I needed to delegate some of my load or drop it altogether.

I explained that the things on my plate—work, family, in-laws—weren't things I could delegate or drop.

"You have to worry about you," he insisted. Then he asked if I liked pancakes.

I answered, "Yes."

"So, what's your favorite topping then?"

"I like syrup."

He went on to tell me that I should find the tallest mountain in the tallest mountain range in India. Then, when I find it, to find the tallest maple tree atop that mountain. And he said, "Climb to the very top of that maple tree and there you will find the very best maple syrup for your pancakes."

I laughed at his silly but caring comments. He scheduled me for ultrasound treatment on my neck to loosen up the muscles, which helped the numbness in my arms to go away. I was relieved that I could continue to work—and maintain my independence.

Near the end of my desensitization therapy with Tim, he reminded me of two truths: I am worthy, and I have a right to be my own person. Throughout the years, he'd taught that you teach people how to treat you by what you tolerate. Also, if you're unsure whether someone's motives are in your best interest or not, test them. If they aren't in your best interest, don't buy into it. If that person doesn't like it, so what; you can only be the victim if you care. For the first time in my life, I had to implement all of those.

The "step away" from my in-laws had turned into two years. During that time—on our own terms—Matt and I muddled through our busy lives of fulfilling demanding jobs and raising five very different boys. Although slightly less than before, Matt continued to shield his heart in case of catastrophe, which created a subtle wedge between us. I knew I'd have to eventually reintegrate with my in-laws. The day that I did, aware of my triggers, I pulled into Matt's parents' driveway in my little white Jeep only to find the entire parking area covered in white vehicles—large four-wheel drive trucks down to small, economical sedans. It seemed that everyone in the family now owned a white rig. Feeling like a little white speck, vowing never to allow myself to become vulnerable to them again, I carried on.

Wayne and
Maggie Osbin,
circa 1975.

Teresa, Brian,
and Lori, 1968.

Lori and
Bobbi, 1968.

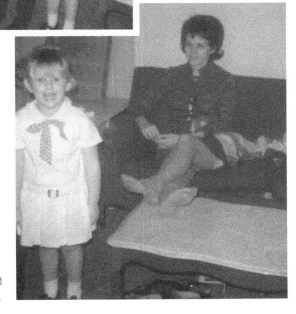

Jenny playing in Grandma and Grandpa's backyard, 1974.

Lori, 1976.

Teresa, 1976.

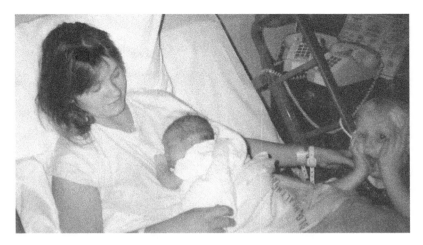

Jenny with sons Tony and Zack, 1991.

Jenny, Tony, and
Zack. London, 2000.

Jenny (center) with sisters Debbie (left) and Penny (right), 2010.

Matt & Jenny's wedding, 2002. Top row, left to right: Son
Thomas, bridesmaid Amy, Jenny, Matt, sons Matthew and Zack.
Bottom row, left to right: Sons Tony and Taylor.

Jenny with father Ivan.   Jenny with mother Bobbi.

Nick, Marie,
and Kasey, 2014.

Kasey (left) and
Nick (right) at
Disneyland, 2014.

Jenny with sons Zack (left)
and Tony (right), 2014.

Matt—*my* fireman—fleeing the Wall Fire on 7-8-17.

CHAPTER TEN

THE OTHER SIDE
OF THE BAR

*The child who once screamed bloody murder when
her mom passed through courtroom doors now worked
on the other side of the same five days a week...*

T he "bar" can mean a lot of things, but in the courtroom, it is the wooden divider that separates the area where cases are tried, or the "well," from the audience. Generally, you are not allowed to pass through the bar until you have *passed the bar* exam—that is, unless you're a court reporter. After licking my wounds from bombing that interview for the official's position back in 2001 and healing from the post-marital ones triggered by my in-laws, I decided I wanted to give the courthouse another try. First, though, seeking confidence, I explored reenrolling at Butte College to finish my degree. Per the academic counselor, with just a few more classes, I could not only complete my A.S. in Court Reporting, but also earn an A.S. in Applied Arts. With the convenience of online courses, I could complete one or two classes each semester around work and family obligations, which is exactly what I did.

I was on my way, and Mom was on a roll. Within her plethora of post-stroke medications—that now included methadone—was Ambien, which caused her to sleepwalk—I mean drive. She vaguely recalled the incident that led to her arrest but said that night a cat had been incessantly mourning underneath her and Billy Jack's car and disturbing their rest. Her intention was simply to start the vehicle and rev its engine to scare the feline away. Instead, when she floored it, she went barreling backward, through two fences, and landed across the street in the neighbor's front yard. Luckily, nobody was injured, including the cat, but Mom was arrested for reckless driving and driving under the influence of, well, Ambien, and spent the night in jail. Several court appearances later, she pled to the reckless driving and was placed on three years of informal probation. The DUI was dismissed.

Mom loathed having to deal with the criminal justice system and had had her fill of nearby neighbors with fences. With the rise in the real estate market and contractors flipping houses, she and Billy Jack sold their home in town and rented a ramshackle trailer in Berry Creek, a mountain community like Concow, only smaller. They were happy in their new place just outside of Oroville...until the money they'd received from the sale ran out. Once they were broke, Mom was miserable. These were the worst conditions I had ever seen her in—the living room floor was so rotten that in certain spots you could see the ground beneath the trailer. Back in the 1990s, she and Billy Jack had lived in a home that was so bad that it had an outhouse—but at least that one had a floor.

The last thing I wanted was to run into my mom on the other side of the bar! When she had no further appearances on her criminal case—so long as she didn't violate probation—I gave the courthouse a call. Much to my surprise, after speaking with the supervising court reporter, I was immediately scheduled in on a pro-tem basis.

Working within the well, each day I received a crash course in a different courtroom. The alpha (-betical) calendars—simply two courtrooms that divided the defendants up alphabetically— were grueling and fast. Hearing about 150 cases a day in either of them, I quickly became familiar with the local attorneys, lingo, code sections, and myriad crimes. Matters heard in the confidential child dependency courtroom were also quick, but often emotionally charged and intense, which made my job doubly exhausting. The juvenile hall calendar was informal and easy to report, as were the collaborative treatment courts—Drug Court, California's Proposition 36, Domestic Violence Court, and H.I.D.E. (High Intensity DUI Enforcement) Court. In no time, I was reporting jury trials, ranging anywhere from drug charges to murder, which were demanding and stressful. My new job was challenging, but I loved it.

Buried in work, long calendar days and court transcripts, I unintentionally skipped out on Mom for Thanksgiving. I'd hosted many holiday dinners for my family—Mom, Billy Jack, and whoever else wanted to come—over the years, but the one the year before had honestly ended quite "bluntly." I didn't allow smoking in my home, so immediately after eating two days' worth of my cooking, everybody left—to enjoy a joint! Mom did help with a quick cleanup beforehand. This year was Matt's turn to spend Thanksgiving with his family—his parents and siblings—and I neglected to communicate that to Mom. The day before the holiday, she called me. In her cracking, on-the-verge-of-crying voice, she said: "Jenny, you know Billy Jack has never been a good provider." Then, in embarrassment, she trailed off, "We don't have anything for dinner tomorrow." I got a fierce knot in my stomach and offered to pack her some food that included a turkey. She said her oven didn't work but she could cook it on the woodstove. Mom knew how to "rough it" better than anyone I'd ever known. Matt and I met my parents on the side of the road at a turnout near their house in Berry Creek. Mom gingerly took the box of food; Billy Jack didn't lift a finger.

Mom had made a comeback after her stroke—my wedding pictures proved it—but after that gut-wrenching Thanksgiving that haunts me still today I noticed her physical and mental health begin to decline. The first sign of the downturn was her baggy clothing; Mom was losing weight. Then, during a flare-up of her COPD, she was hospitalized. The day I visited her, she was delirious and thought the nurses were going to kill her. She didn't even recognize who I was at first. When she came to, she was dying for a cigarette. Since I didn't smoke, she recited my stepbrother Ronny's wife's phone number and insisted that I call and ask her to bring her one. I did so. In the days following Mom's hospitalization, her weight continued to drop and her depression worsened.

At work, I received word that one of the official reporters was retiring and that the court would be posting to fill the upcoming vacancy. I felt I had a good chance of getting the position and was stoked about it. That very night, while making dinner for my family, Mom happened to call. She sounded "up" and in the mood to chat, which seemed odd. I assumed she'd just gotten a refill on her meds. I told her the good news about the job opening. In a slightly elevated tone, like she was happy for me, she said, "That's great." Then, in a flat tone—not sad, not excited—accompanied by some sort of chuckle, like she was embarrassed to bring it up, she said, "Jenny, you know, I just want to tell you that—you know, I'm not going to live forever—there's a place in Pennsylvania that studies bodies of people who have abused drugs. They'll take care of picking me up and everything. I want to know if you'll donate my body to them when I die so that they can study it and learn the effects of drugs on your organs and stuff. You know, I've taken drugs all my life; maybe they can use my body to help people."

"I'm not going to do that," I said, "you want to be cremated."

"I know, but I just don't want to be a burden on anybody with a funeral and everything."

"You're not going to be a burden, Mom. I love you." Down from my high about the new job opportunity, we got off the phone.

I wasn't the only one noticing changes in Mom. Sam, now expecting, and Kevin were in town visiting. After seeing her, Sam called me crying: "Aunt Jenny, Grandma won't eat, and she's lost a lot of weight. She just sleeps all day on the couch. She's giving up." Putting two and two together, the only reason I could fathom why Mom would give up is because all my nieces and nephews she had raised were either grown and out of the house or on their way. I believed, facing an empty nest, my mom was losing her will to live. December of that same year, 2006, Sam gave birth to my great-nephew Kasey, a handsome baby boy with hazel eyes and perfect blond curls, a great-grandson who would never get to meet his great-grandma.

On a Wednesday evening in January of 2007, Mom called again: "Jenny, I'm going crazy up here [in Berry Creek]. Do you think you can help me find a place in town to rent? I can pay up to $600 a month."

Annoyed about unrelated matters that were going on in my life at that time, and not thinking for a minute she was serious about moving to town, I said, "Sure," in a tone that I wish I had never used. I wasn't mean, but I was short with her. I would have done anything for my mom to have a comfortable life, but she always chose otherwise—she always chose less for herself. No matter what, though, I still loved her.

Exactly one week after that Wednesday phone call, I picked up the newspaper that evening to see if there were any rentals I could help Mom and Billy Jack move into. I looked at properties and mobile homes for sale that I could even possibly buy and let them live in. In the middle of that night, I got another call. It was my step-aunt.

"Jenny, your mom's gone."

"What?"

"Yes. I'm sorry. She's gone. The ambulance has already taken her away." My step-aunt explained that all Billy Jack knew was that Mom had gone to bed early that night because she wasn't feeling well. He went to check on her, and she wasn't breathing.

I was crushed.

I knew Mom would die someday, but I hadn't expected her to be so young—eight days from her sixtieth birthday. Just like I had told her, her funeral expenses weren't a burden. I paid to have her cremated after the autopsy, which is what I knew she really wanted—not to be donated to a lab in Pennsylvania. My brother Brian later reimbursed me half the cost.

Within mere days of Mom's passing, I was leaving work at lunch when, lo and behold, I saw Jonny, wearing a baby blue suit, standing with a group of people in the rotunda of the courthouse. The once aspiring fireman seemed to always be near during my times of trouble—like when our house was raided, when Mom told me about my real father, when I was trying to leave Rick, and when Lori passed—but as soon as I saw him, I put on my blinders. He turned to watch me leave the courthouse. That's when I figured it out: you should always follow your heart, but you must use your head to guide and protect it.

The court was scheduling interviews for the official court reporter position. Mine was set on the Tuesday before Mom's birthday. I remember feeling relieved that I wasn't going to have to hold it together on what was bound to be a painful day. Then the phone rang: "Jenny, we're going to have to move your interview to Thursday, January twenty-fifth, at nine o'clock."

Wonderful. I have to interview on her birthday. With a broken heart, even with the year of court experience I now had under my belt, I didn't know if I could pull it off. My worst fear was that I'd bomb it again.

When January 25 arrived, the interviewing panel was aware that it was my mom's birthday and that she had just died. In low spirits, but thankfully without tears, I did my best to competently answer their questions. When it was over, I felt good about what I'd done, but figured that whatever was supposed to happen, would happen. I continued working per diem while I waited for the outcome.

One afternoon, when court had recessed for the day, I was called into the supervising court reporter's office. A person from administration met me there and said, "Jenny, we'd like to offer you the job."

Elated, all I could say was, "Really? Oh, my gosh! Thank you so much!"

Happy and feeling proud of myself, I headed out the door to go home. The first person I thought to call was my mother, which of course I couldn't do. I got into my car and started to phone Matt only to find I had a voice message waiting for me. It was the funeral home: "Jenny, your mom's ready to be picked up."

Tears streamed down my cheeks as I drove through town. I took her ashes to my home where we, in the next weeks, had a small family-only memorial for her. I arranged for a pastor to speak at her service, played "Amazing Grace," which was her favorite song, and then we all feasted on fried chicken. Immediately after the gathering, tough guy Billy Jack ran back to his ex-wife, the mother of his children, a woman Mom had always felt was a threat.

As my position within the county moved forward, I was given an office directly behind Courtroom 1 that abutted the noisy elevator. It had been a utility closet, but it was mine now. Designated as "Office 10" by its placard, it also bore "No Admittance" from its earlier use as a closet. That's where administration personnel met with me to go over the long list of rules employees were supposed to follow: "One, you're not to do anything to embarrass the Court."

Stuck at "One," all I could think was: *Are you sure I should be here?*

Having completed my degrees, I could have walked in a bona fide graduation ceremony, like the high school one I missed out on, but instead I opted to have the certificates mailed to me. Now I regret not walking in both. On a wall in the tight quarters of my office, I hung the professionally framed degrees atop one another. I gazed at them often, not to remind myself of where I had started, because that was everywhere—in the courtroom, at home, and on the street—but to remind myself of how far I had come. For that, I was proud.

Along with all the perks of my new job as a government employee—salary, insurance, retirement, paid vacation, and sick days—I worked with a great group of colleagues, most with whom I had attended court-reporting school. I also had an amazing supervisor who didn't get flustered when she had to switch me out of the schedule with a fellow reporter because I had a relative on the calendar whose case I couldn't report, something that happened from time to time.

Three months into my job as an official court reporter, sitting in my office with my head down on my desk, I appreciated the "No Admittance" sign. I was once again sickened by whom I had chosen to father my children and what he was putting them through. Rick, driving drunk on the wrong side of the freeway, had crashed into an oncoming vehicle and caused serious injury to its young occupants. That day, he was sentenced in Courtroom 1 to ten years, four months in state prison for his final DUI. Aside from several months outside of prison before his death when he was granted a compassionate release, prison was where he spent the rest of his life.

Still crushed over my mom's death, staying busy was my refuge; any downtime left me hurting and trying to make sense of her life. She had told me, "If you get an education, nobody can ever take it away from you," yet she never dared to even get her high school diploma. She had dreamt of becoming an architect or writer, yet her entire adulthood was spent dependent on aid. First welfare, then Supplemental Security Income (SSI) for which she'd been approved due to, among other things, "lack of employability." My mom was no dummy, but her entire life had been wasted. *Why?* To add to my confusion, when the autopsy report came in, I was shocked to learn Mom's cause of death. A life-long substance user, if anyone knew how to use, she did. In part, it read:

The body is that of an unembalmed white female whose general physical condition is consistent with the indicated age of fifty-nine years. The body weighs an estimated 110 pounds and the estimated body length is sixty-three to sixty-four inches.
Located over the right upper medial breast is a small apparent

"K" tattoo letter (actually, it had faded, and it was the initials
"JR," for Junior, her fourth husband). Located over the right
upper lateral scapula is the expression "Solomon's Pleasure."
Cause of death: Acute methadone poisoning.
Other significant conditions: Severe Chronic Obstructive Pul-
monary Disease
Bipolar Disorder
Atherosclerotic Heart Disease
Intracerebral hemorrhage, 2001
Seizure disorder
History of polysubstance abuse
Recent marijuana use
Toxicology: Methadone = 0.71 mg/L
Cannabinoids—positive
Delta-9-THC 13 ng/ml; Delta-9-Cooh 82 ng/ml.

Cause of death: acute methadone poisoning; otherwise
known as an overdose.

The child who once screamed bloody murder when her mom
passed through courtroom doors now worked on the other side
of the same five days a week. Broken over the recent loss of my
mother, I tried to reconcile with the past, but I couldn't escape
the reminders. The first, in the alpha court, was what could have
been my very own reflection: a big-eyed young woman with long,
brown, ratty hair. Seemingly out of place in her orange jail clothing, she wasn't loud and obnoxious, but timid and scared. Looking at four years in prison for felony drug charges, she was about

to enter a plea of *nolo contendre*. In my gut I knew how easily I could have ended up in her shoes, wearing orange. I was grateful for the road, albeit a difficult one, I'd chosen.

In the CPS courtroom, I heard cases involving infants being born tox-positive; children, many with multiple dads—alleged or bio, and presumed—with PTSD, attachment disorders, and/or sexually acting out. Most of the kids had been removed from their families for issues stemming from parental substance use: neglect, physical or emotional abuse. *Would I have been better off if I'd been removed from my family as a child?* I loved them, so I always settled on no. Now, had someone intervened early on and helped my mom, that would have helped all of us. The way things turned out, my family was being removed from *me*.

The juvenile hall, where I could have landed years ago while running amok in Concow, was full of minors who had drug-addicted, AWOL parents. The fortunate ones had grandparents, aunts, uncles, older siblings, and/or caring adults looking after them; others didn't. There's not a more disappointing face than the one of a minor who is free to be released from juvie, yet back on the courtroom calendar the following week because nobody showed to pick him or her up.

Many kids in the hall were there because of crimes they'd committed for their gang "families." A twelve-year-old Sureno female involved in a drive-by shooting. A fifteen-year-old Norteno male who had stabbed an innocent person. They didn't know it, but their "families" and mine weren't all that different. All answered to someone/something else—a shot caller or a substance—lived in a cage, and lost loved ones.

Then there was Drug Court. Offenders on this calendar were called "participants," not defendants. In addition to a judge, probation officer, deputy district attorney, and defense attorney, this substance-use treatment court included behavioral health counselors. A collaboration between all parties, I saw in them a genuine desire for each participant to succeed in the program and ultimately graduate, and that was beautiful.

To graduate Drug Court, participants had to obtain a job, driver's license, high school diploma or GED, complete substance-use treatment classes, and pay off all their fines and fees. For some, that was a lot to ask. Few participants new to the program came in excited and ready for treatment; most were defiant and thought they could kick their addiction on their own, if they even admitted they had one. In the end, they either graduated and exited through the front door to society and a better life or through the back door to one of the alpha calendars.

Growing up within a family of substance users, I thought I'd seen it all, but this courtroom proved me wrong time and time again, especially during the "violation of probation" cases.

There was the middle-aged man, with a burned face, on calendar for a dirty (meth) test, his oxygen tank in tow and its tube running over his beard and up into his nostrils. The judge asked, "Are you smoking meth or shooting it up?" Quietly he replied, "No, ma'am, I ain't shootin'." By the burns on his face, that was obvious.

Or the adamant young woman who claimed to have kicked her alcohol addiction on her own. "It's just so amazing," she said, "I did it all by myself." When asked how long she had been sober, she answered, "Since thirteen days from now." Before being remanded for showing up to court under the influence of alcohol for the third time, the judge hit her with the truth: "You've obviously got something really deep down inside hurting you."

There was a woman, well into her pregnancy, on calendar for a violation of probation; she'd had the police called on her. She said she'd come home and found the father of her unborn baby in bed with another woman. When asked what happened, she simply said, "I socked him." The behavioral health counselor precisely summed it up: "She has a broken 'picker.' Her 'picker' is broken." It was suggested that the participant look for a new partner.

When the judge ordered a prison-bound defendant to have no contact with his co-defendant ex-girlfriend, as she was finally on track and doing quite well in treatment, he became irate and called the judge every expletive under the sun. The bailiff escorted him out of the courtroom through the side door. The judge, a true professional, held her composure, but even judges are human, and we had to take a short break to regroup.

Then there was the woman with two felonies who tried to embrace treatment but struggled to stay clean. The big, bad-turned-soft deputy district attorney encouraged her. Teary-eyed, he claimed if she could just hang in there and prevail over her addiction, he would do whatever he had to, "bend the law, maybe even something illegal," he joked, so she could walk out of court one day a non-felon. (Successful completion of Drug Court allows some felonies to be reduced to misdemeanors.)

Another participant appearing in court for a violation of probation for (of course) meth got some sage advice from the judge, who quoted Paul Simon: "Fifty ways to leave your lover." She suggested, "You just slip out the back, Jack; make a new plan, Stan; you don't need to be coy, Roy, just get yourself free."

And then there was the pregnant woman appearing for a dirty drug test. Addicted to opiates, if she didn't get off the pills, her baby was going to be born addicted, too, and would be removed from her at birth by Children's Services. Heartbreaking...

The best part of Drug Court was seeing the participants after they'd embraced treatment. All were grateful to have been given their lives back. Some said "thank you" outright, others through poems, fantastic spray art, or songs. One day, the judge went so far as to go against security's protocol and allowed a Tim Robbins look-alike to sing Blind Melon's "Change" at her bench for all of us. He said he used to play that song for his late sister; he'd lost her to an overdose. As he strummed his guitar, I sat with a knot in my stomach, immersed in his music. The greatest "thank yous," however, radiated from proud participants who brought in their healthy, drug-free newborns to show off. The judge stepped down from the bench to nestle every single one.

In Drug Court, one of my more memorable participants was a middle-aged male. When his case was called, smiling ear to ear, he made his way to the counsel table. He thanked the judge, probation officer, attorneys, and behavioral health counselors, then explained that everything in his life was in order and going great. He said he'd even gotten a significant raise at work "for no reason at all." At the end of his matter, he asked the judge if his girlfriend could come up to the table with him. The judge said yes. Surprised and a bit embarrassed, his girlfriend slowly walked up the aisle past the bar. The gentleman stood up from his chair, got down on bended knee, pulled out a ring, and proposed marriage to her right in front of everybody.

Shaking, she quietly answered, "Yes."

The two embraced in a big hug, the defense attorney took pictures, and the audience cheered them on. The newly engaged couple walked back down the aisle, receiving congratulations from other Drug Court participants and their families, and then walked through those huge mahogany doors to start a new and better life together. It was amazing!

That proposal was incredible to report, but there are no words to express how I felt the day I watched my first mom graduate the program. The audience portion of the courtroom was half filled with her family. Her young daughter, smiling wide, waved a banner showing how proud she was of her beaming mother—something I had longed to experience for my own mom ever since I was a child. As the judge, probation officer, attorneys, and behavioral health counselors took turns speaking of how pleased they were of the graduate, I quietly stroked my Stenograph machine. As I witnessed a family—and hopefully generations—changed for the better, my eyes welled up and I did my best not to lose it in front of everybody. I'd known it from the day I first stepped into Drug Court: the "bar" in this courtroom was not a line of demarcation, but a bridge—*a bridge over troubled water*—to a better life.

CHAPTER ELEVEN

RUDE AWAKENING

Fourteen hundred forty minutes in a day, and I'd wake up in the middle of the night, look over at the clock, and see 2:22, 3:33, or 4:44...

"**S**o, your mom's gone, huh?" Grandma Maggie asked. Now in her mid-eighties and bed-bound in a care facility in Stockton, I tried to get down to see her as often as I could, but that ended up being only three times during the year Mom died. With Aunt Jeannie succumbing to lung cancer—after surviving breast cancer—seven years prior, Grandma had outlived both her daughters. I can't begin to describe how empty the look in her eyes was as she waited for my response about Mom. All I could do was nod my head.

The three visits I had managed to squeeze in with Grandma were golden. She'd tell stories of our family history; I'd catch myself leaning over the metal railing of her hospital bed, like a young child, tuned in. Her eyes lit up whenever she spoke of

Grandpa Wayne. She said they were married in his parents' backyard in Oklahoma in 1941, and after she gave birth to my Aunt Jeannie, they moved to California to be near her parents, who had migrated there in a covered wagon. "Your grandpa's family was quite hot about it." She laughed.

Speaking of Grandpa, I told her how he wanted nothing to do with me as a baby.

She said, "Oh, no. Grandpa was stubborn, but he warmed up to you. You would ride all over with him in his pickup."

"I don't remember that at all, Grandma," I said. "I remember his Ford Courier, but not him warming up to me—ever."

Probing into what she might remember about Mom's relationship with my dad, I asked her about him. She said, "Your grandpa despised him. He went to your dad's house one time to check on your mom and was threatened by him with a hammer."

Unclear which dad she was talking about, I asked, "Willy or Ivan?"

She obviously knew about as much as I did about my fathers, because she had to stop and think for a moment. She finally answered, "Willy."

Grandma once told me, "I may be old-fashioned, but I believe there's only one man for every woman." She held true to that because Grandpa died twenty-nine years before her, and I never heard her speak of another man. The day before what would have been my fourth visit to see her, I got a call that she'd peacefully left us. I could have kicked myself, because I had originally planned on visiting her the day of the call.

I attended a lovely graveside service for Grandma that was

held at Cherokee Memorial, the cemetery that holds generations of my mom's side of the family. After the closing prayer, a relative tossed a pack of Hubba Bubba bubble gum into the plot. Those of us who understood why smiled through the tears. Grandma was buried right next to Grandpa in a casket lined in deep purple, her favorite color.

Before Mom died, she gave me four boxes full of Grandma's cookbooks and photo albums filled with newspaper and magazine clippings of favorite recipes. After Grandma passed, I found an envelope dated June 15, 1966, among her books. It was from Aunt Jeannie and addressed to Grandma and Grandpa in Seminole, Oklahoma. Inside the envelope was an anniversary card. Inside the anniversary card, there was an impression of a quarter that had once been there to represent their twenty-five-year silver anniversary. It must have been dated 1941 because Aunt Jeannie wrote: "I think that was the only 1941 quarter they made. I didn't think I was going to find one."

———

With the loss of both Mom and Grandma, 2007 was a tough year, but in 2008 the circle of life continued when Sam became pregnant again. She was scared that another child would be too much too soon, but I assured her that she had a good husband who loved her, my help, and everything would be okay. Nine months later, she and Kevin were blessed with another handsome boy, my great-nephew Nick, born with brown eyes and straight, blond hair. Still striving to work hard and live a drug-free life, Kevin was the wage earner of his family while Sam was a homemaker and remarkable mom. Their boys were a priority and well taken care of. I was a proud aunt.

Just as the circle of life continued, so did the circle of work. Business was booming at the courthouse, and I was assigned to jury trial after jury trial. When the Concow Cannabis Coalition got busted for a marijuana garden that pushed the envelope within the Compassionate Use Act and the Medical Marijuana Program Act, their case—involving my old stomping ground—landed in my courtroom. Although awkward for me, it was quite entertaining.

Following the People's case in chief, as if playing their role in a skit produced by the *Saturday Night Live* cast, by way of a grant of immunity, thirteen members of the Concow Cannabis Coalition collective testified on behalf of the defendant. A young adult male, not taking the situation seriously, wore a T-shirt that read, "It's all fun and games until the cops show up." Boy, was the hard-nosed prosecutor amused when she read it into the record. With a newspaper reporter present, the defense attorney, shaking his head, muttered, "Is this going to be in the paper?"

Of course, it was.

A second member testified right after having "medicated." Slowly, he made his way to the witness stand. Not surprisingly, he couldn't remember anything. Plus, he spoke so softly that everyone, including myself seated right next to him, had to repeatedly ask him to restate his answers. The prosecutor stepped to the far end of the courtroom to force him to elevate his voice, but to no avail.

Another collective member, a twenty-two-year-old, testified under oath that he had originally been given a medical marijuana recommendation at age thirteen. The judge whispered under his breath, "Must have been from his pediatrician."

After all the members had testified—each related in spirit if not by blood—the defendant, the so-called "cannabis consultant" of the collective, took the stand. In his late twenties, he was adamant that the members of the Concow Cannabis Coalition were content with "living off the land," growing their "medicine" to share with their "fellow mankind out of compassion," and, a bit disturbing to me, even "starting up a young work force." He testified that his role was to "over-stand" the collective. When questioned about what he meant by that term, he got flustered and animated and said it means he would "dance on the plants; do the plant dance."

Huh?

After a nine-day trial, the jury acquitted the defendant on the cultivation charge. I gather that they believed, as did I, he truly was in it for his "medicine."

I was barreling through pages and pages of appeal transcripts when I got a call from my stepmom, Pat: "Jenn, Dad is in jail. He has to get help, or I'm done with him!"

When Dad retired in 2006, he lost any sort of schedule to adhere to regarding his beer consumption; instead of waiting until the end of the workday to catch a buzz, the day began and ended with one. He stopped taking trips with Pat to Tahoe or Vegas like they'd done in the past. Pat, also retired, refused to sit at home and, making the most of her retirement, went on excursions solo. At times, she'd be gone a full one to two weeks. Dad wouldn't eat when she was away, only drink his beloved beer. His carelessness caused a drastic decline in his mental health and exacerbated his other medical conditions, including the neuropathy in his feet. After undergoing vascular surgery, the doctor even warned him: "Ivan, if you don't stop drinking, we may end up having to amputate a leg." Still, Dad was too stubborn to, and by his third year in retirement, it caught up to him.

On the day of Dad's arraignment, I drove the three hours to the Calaveras County Superior Court in San Andreas. While waiting for court to begin, I listened to the deputy joke with staff about "the old guy [my dad] in the walker," and how while walking him from the jail to the holding cell, he told him, "Just don't piddle on me now." Annoyed, I sat on the other side of the bar thinking to myself, *Lucky for that deputy I work in a courthouse, too, and I know what it means to be jaded.* I let it go.

Dad was charged with PC 591, damaging phone or electrical line, a misdemeanor. Pat, who was still a drinker, had threatened to call the police during an argument, so Dad pulled the phone cord out of the wall. The judge ordered Dad to stay away from Pat and their home, then sentenced him to thirty days of residential rehab. A glutton for punishment, I delivered him to an alcohol treatment facility Pat found in Sonora that accepted their insurance and made the four-hour drive each way every weekend for a visit. It was exhausting. At the rehab, Dad was diagnosed with severe alcohol-induced dementia and told to quit drinking or he wouldn't live another two years. He finally complied.

After Dad's thirty days of rehabilitation were up, he couldn't go home because of the restraining order, so he came to stay with me. That lasted a month. In one of his demented rages, he nearly set out by way of his neuropathic feet and walker back to his home with Pat in Valley Springs—a two-and-a-half-hour drive. I couldn't work and watch him, so Pat reluctantly agreed to let him back in. I thanked the heavens above.

With Dad situated under his own roof again—*Hallelujah!*—I was in my office binding the first volume of a bulky appeal when I received shocking news: Brooke, the strongest girl I knew, had succumbed to sleep apnea. She was just thirty-seven years young—my age. It was surreal: my teenage bestie's life was over, and I hadn't even lived yet, at least not for myself. My years had been spent fulfilling the needs and desires of others—Mom, Rick, my children (rightly so), and Dad. In the middle of binding the second volume, I was hit with an epiphany: *What about my needs and desires? When do I get to put them front and center? First in line instead of last? When do I get my turn?* Before the third and final volume was bound, I'd figured things out. Of Matt's and my five sons, the older three had graduated from high school and were on their own—Matthew married to his love and Zack engaged to be—and our younger two were set to graduate the following June. With an empty nest on the horizon, my turn to have my needs and desires front and center was right around the bend. I poised myself accordingly.

Sam and Kevin were still doing amazing, except when it came to their weight. Upon quitting drugs years earlier, they had gained a good amount, then after Sam had the boys, she and Kevin put on even more. On the edge of obesity, they both decided to undergo bariatric surgery. Matt warned them of recent research he'd read suggesting that marital problems can arise after a procedure like that and spoke of his good friend whose wife had undergone one. "Exactly a year after her bypass, the couple separated," he said with concern in his voice. Sam and Kevin reassured us that their marriage was solid and there was nothing to worry about.

Life continued moving forward for all of us, and before I knew it, Matt's and my two younger sons, among the Class of 2010, graduated high school. It was a bittersweet milestone for my husband and me. On one hand, we had to say our goodbyes to years of muddy football games, prom nights, and the not-so-spectacular boundary-setting battles we experienced with each of our five sons; on the other, although we'd forever hold tightly to all of them and provide for their future as needed, we'd get to enjoy one another outside of child rearing. I was stoked: it was almost my turn.

Zack married his love on 10-10-10. Sam and Kevin, along with their young sons, pulled up to the country club venue that morning in a beautiful silver Chrysler 300. A stunning Sam stepped out of the car in the little black dress she said she'd bought specifically for the event. As the family walked along the windy sidewalk, Kevin, slimmed down in black as well, held Nick in his arms while Kasey galumphed alongside his mother. Their surgeries had been successful; Sam and Kevin looked fantastic and as happy as ever.

Something I'd always wanted to do but couldn't afford was to invest in a rental property, or maybe even flip one. With a downed real estate market and our last two teenagers out of school and working, I thought it would be a great time to give it a shot.

However, instead of a rental, what I found was a diamond in-the-rough foreclosure in exactly the area I had wanted to retire one day. Located in mountainous eastern Oroville, the house was only ten miles from my work. On top of having a great location, its price had dropped a whopping $85,000, which put it in our range. I phoned Matt, we met to look at it, then made a full-price offer. When it was accepted, we were ecstatic. We decided to make our current home the rental.

Matt and I were still living in our old house when Sam and Kevin dropped in, this time showing up in a full-size Titan truck. They both had lost a lot of weight—too much weight—from their surgeries. At least I thought so. They were standing with us in the kitchen when Sam inquired, "Aunt Jenny and Uncle Matt, we want to ask that if something happens to us, will you guys take care of our boys?" She looked at me and said, "You have just the right amount of kindness," then looked at Matt, "You have just the right amount of firmness."

Kevin added, "We have a million-dollar life insurance policy."

Perplexed, but thinking they were just looking out for their kids' wellbeing, Matt nodded his head in the affirmative, and I said, "Yes. Of course, we'll take care of the boys if something happens to you."

Matt and I received the keys to our new place on my mom's birthday in January, but we didn't move in until March. Not surprisingly, our two youngest sons elected to find roommates and a place in town rather than relocate with us to the outskirts of Oroville. With all five of our adult children out of the house and on their own, Matt and I were bona fide empty nesters in a three-bedroom, three-bath, three-level stick-built house that sat on seven acres along a proposed scenic highway. Driving to and from our home, we could see over all of Oroville. Viewing the city's lights at nighttime was spectacular. As a bonus, we had a seasonal stream and a view of the coastal mountain range from our kitchen window.

Excited to get started making our house our home, Matt cleared brush for fire protection while I painted the interior neutral colors that complemented our mountain surroundings. We replaced old condensation-filled double-pane windows, started devising a plan to replace the dry-rotted deck, and researched exterior siding materials and colors.

For landscaping, I planted paint-by-number style predesigned drought-tolerant and deer-resistant flower gardens. The successful plantings (that survived my lack of having a green thumb) were Russian sage, fountain grass, hollyhocks, a butterfly bush, and tickseed. The black-eyed Susans refused to grow inside the garden's perimeter yet thrived just outside—kind of like me. I attempted to add my favorite shrub, the beautiful Matilija poppy—aka "Fried Egg Plant" or "Showgirl"—to our landscape. To grow it from seed meant to subject it to fire, like burning a pile of pine needles overtop, as it will only shoot if triggered by smoke—which is why it was my favorite. That approach being much too complicated for this novice, I opted to simply transplant the poppy into the ground. However, it lay dormant for months, and then died. (Three springs later, Matt took it upon himself to attempt a transplant of the Matilija again—into a heart-shaped hole he'd dug for it. It was a success.)

Busy working in the gardens, I met Bobo, an Anna's hummingbird. With a hot-pink head and green body, the mighty little creature—and only bird capable of flying backward—would visit me most anywhere I was on the property. Often perched on a tiny branch right outside of our kitchen window, I set him up with his very own feeder. When it was empty, he'd make me aware by a face-to-face shudder-in-place that said, "Hello? I'm hungry!" One afternoon, I heard a commotion outside. I found Bobo, along with a group of hummers, taking dives at a garter snake that was making its way up a pine tree, probably seeking nests for a meal of birds' eggs. The snake couldn't withstand the attack and dropped to the ground and slithered off.

I also met Dottie Mae, a stray schnauzer-terrier mix who wandered into our yard. Given how loyal she turned out to be, I almost named her Daisy Mae, II, after my childhood pal. While enjoying a cup of coffee one Saturday morning, I spotted her, skittish and scared, eying me from beneath some bushes. Coated in burrs and with a left front paw that was worn raw, it appeared she had covered a lot of ground on her own. She was so wary of people, I could barely coax her into taking a bath, but after hours of removing stickers from her wiry gray and white coat, she began to trust me and soon became my protector. Until she learned she could trust Matt, too, she'd let out a low "grrr" that made him think twice about getting too close to me too quickly.

There's a downside to everything, including our living in a mountain retreat. One part was the miserable systemic poison oak I got that year that required steroids to beat. The other was the not-so-grand view of our neighbor's pot garden from our master bedroom window. As harvest season approached, the tent-stakers came, which I'd learned from working in a court-room were often armed with weapons and dogs to guard the valuable commodity. Being so close to home—in more ways than one—it was a bit unnerving.

———

Empty nesters, Matt and I decided to celebrate my big four-oh by way of a spur-of-the-moment trip to Fort Bragg, California. As if we were a teenage couple, we perused the tide pools, combed the beaches for sand dollars, and enjoyed the vibrant yet soothing sunsets. Like we'd never done it before, we even dressed up for a fancy dinner at a pricy restaurant. We *hadn't* done it before. I had so much fun that weekend that upon our arrival home I made a promise to myself: "It's finally my turn; come hell or high water, I'm not giving it up again." I even boldly whispered, "Bring it on."

Well, if you want to hear God laugh, tell him your plans, right? The Saturday before Easter of 2012, I was on my way down to visit Dad in Valley Springs. While I was fueling up my car, Kevin called. He was crying and upset. Afraid, I asked him what was wrong. He said that Sam had fallen out of their truck—while he was driving—and that she had been holding Nick in her arms when she fell. Aside from road rash that, like an apple, had peeled an approximate two-inch strip of hair and scalp off Nick's tiny head, CT scans showed that he was going to be okay. However, Sam's skull was fractured, and doctors were monitoring the swelling of her brain. Without hesitating, I drove directly to the hospital, which was about an hour southwest of Dad's place. I waited through the evening, until the doctor confirmed that the swelling had stabilized, and I knew Sam would be okay. I stayed at Dad's that night, arriving home on Easter Day to a full holiday feast prepared by my immediate family. How amazing it felt to be cared for!

Sam spent several days in the hospital before the cerebral swelling subsided enough for her release. Still in a great amount of discomfort, she was sent home with a prescription for opioid pain meds. Sam also suffered hearing loss in her left ear because of the fall, which threw off her equilibrium and made her unstable when she stood or walked.

How does someone fall out of a truck while it is being driven? Per Kevin, "I was parked and facing uphill in a highway turnout. When I stepped on the gas to get back on the road, Sam was leaning against the door, and the baby's blanket must have been caught in it, because it opened and they fell out." Most people thought the story sounded bogus and that it involved domestic violence. I disagreed: Sam would never allow herself to be abused.

Valley Springs, where Dad lived, and Farmington, where Sam lived, were only thirty minutes apart. In the weeks following my niece's injury, whenever I could, I'd make the drive to see both. Surprisingly, Dad was remaining sober, and getting along with Pat. That put me at ease. Kevin, too, was holding things together— his work, taking care of Sam, who slept most of the time while recovering, and their boys. On one visit to Sam's, Kasey and Nick, as rambunctious as ever, were jumping on the couch and glued to cartoons; they appeared unaffected by their family's difficulties. On another, they dragged me over to their garden to show me the very first strawberry of the season. I was worried for Sam and Kevin, with everything they were facing, but they seemed to be making it through.

Back at home, as the days passed, I noticed myself constantly checking the time. Freakishly, more often than not, it would be exactly 2:22, 3:33, 4:44, or 5:55. Fourteen hundred forty minutes in a day, and I'd wake up in the middle of the night, look over at the clock, and see 2:22, 3:33, or 4:44 a.m. Oddly enough, it took me back in time, to Grandma Maggie's living room floor, when I sang along, "444-5555, that's the number of the Classified." But who in the hell was left to call? I told Matt how weird it was.

He laughed, "Just as long as it isn't 11:11."

"But sometimes it is."

CHAPTER TWELVE

OF TWEAKERS AND ZOMBIES

"Aunt Jenny, my dad's taking so long because he's working hard so he can buy us a castle..."

O f my childhood family, Grandma Maggie, Mom, and Lori were no longer with us, and the last I'd heard, Teresa was living under a bridge somewhere in Stockton. The succeeding generation of my nieces and nephews was spread out. I had regular contact with most of them—Sam, Stephanie, Steven, and Stanley—but I hadn't seen Amber or Christina (who disappointingly was homeless alongside her mother Teresa) in years. Missing my kin, I decided to host the upcoming Thanksgiving holiday dinner for my side of the family—Grandma Maggie-style. I contacted everyone I could, and they were all open to it. Sam joked, "We'll be there, as long as you make your banana cream pie!" Of course, I would.

During the months after Sam's fall, if I called and caught her when she was awake, she usually sounded chipper; however, I could tell her recovery was progressing slowly. Given her equilibrium issues, she would often be in bed or on the couch while we spoke. Sometimes she'd be playing with her boys, and I'd hear their laughter in the background. Sometimes she'd be trying to correct them, and I'd still hear their laughter in the background—because they rarely took her seriously.

According to Sam, Kevin was doing quite well holding down the fort, but once bill collectors started calling my home looking for them, I discovered that wasn't true. When I passed along the agencies' information and spoke with Sam about their finances, she became upset and explained, "Yeah, Kevin's been waiting for weeks for his boss to pay him." Then, "Yeah, Kevin is looking for another job because his boss *won't* pay him." In one of our last conversations, she said that Kevin was all decked out in a brand-new suit on his way to interview for a new position. I assumed the couple was only struggling financially, and I was hopeful that it would pass, but along with the bill collectors, soon the SPCA called, too. A good Samaritan had found their family dog running down the road but couldn't hold her for long. I passed that information on to Sam and Kevin, but suddenly, all communication stopped. At first, if their voice mail wasn't full, I'd leave messages, but they wouldn't return my calls. Then their phones were disconnected. The bill collectors kept leaving nasty messages with me, and the SPCA concerned ones.

Thanksgiving's turnout was a small my-side-of-the-family gathering, with no word from either Sam or Kevin, even though they'd told me they would be there. Finally, in December I heard from Sam. For the first time ever, she asked to borrow money from me. She said they would pay me back when Kevin got his check, which was supposed to be right before Christmas. I wired her the cash without question. Christmas came and went. I didn't hear from them again for six months.

At 3:00 a.m. on a Wednesday, my phone rang. It was Sam. A police officer had let her use his personal cell phone.

In a hysterical state, she said, "Aunt Jenny, the cops are harassing me. They say if I don't get my kids to bed they're going to call Child Protective Services."

Half asleep, bewildered, and upset about her predicament, I groaned, "It's three in the morning, how come your kids are not in their bed?"

She answered, "We are eating at a restaurant; they want to close, but Kevin can't find his wallet to get a room. Please, can you get a room for us? I'll pay you back. They are going to take my kids away."

Still trying to understand her situation, I asked, "Where is Kevin? Are you guys fighting? Did you leave him?"

"No, no, I don't know where he went. He walked off down the road."

"Fine. Let me look online and see if I can find you a room. What's the phone number and address?"

She gave me the information I needed, and I turned on the computer and found a nearby motel. Sam and Kevin were living in Sacramento at the time. I had no idea why they weren't at their home. Once I had promised to fax a copy of my credit card

and driver's license by 8:00 a.m. that morning, the motel attendant agreed to let them stay.

I called the number Sam gave me for the restaurant, but they
had already left. Through caller ID, I reached the officer on his
cell phone. He said he had dropped them off at a twenty-four-
hour restaurant and explained that Sam and her family had been
evicted from their home earlier that day and had nowhere to go.

Frustrated, I said, "Why didn't she just tell me that?" I told
the officer that I could rent them a room, and where it would
be. He graciously went back, picked them up, and delivered
them there.

Once she'd arrived at the motel, Sam thanked me and said
she'd call in the morning to explain everything.

Well, morning came and went, and she never called; but at
checkout, the motel attendant did, wanting to know if there was
authorization for them to stay a second night.

"Absolutely not."

"I didn't think so," she replied.

I heard nothing more until four months later, on October 8,
2012, when I got another call, this time from my nephew Steven's
wife: "Aunt Jenny, Sam's kids are with CPS. They've had them for
five days!"

I realized later that five days before would have been my
birthday. Happy birthday, right? With a knot in my stomach, I
asked, "What? Why? Where?"

"I don't know, but they're here in town."

"Okay. I'll see what I can find out."

My great-nephews—Kasey and Nick—now age five and four,

had been detained by Child Protective Services and were in an emergency shelter because Sam and Kevin had left them unattended with a roommate for days. After my further investigation through family members, I learned that apparently Sam and Kevin were using drugs, and Sam had an outstanding arrest warrant for possession of controlled substances. I couldn't believe it. The CPS matter was under the jurisdiction of the courthouse where I worked—*lovely*. To step in meant that I would have to reveal my anomalous background to social workers, attorneys, and the Court—all people I worked with. Talk about blowing your cover. Still, knowing that Sam and Kevin were visiting Kasey and Nick daily at the shelter, and not thinking the outcome of the situation would lead to anything other than reuniting my niece's family, I opted to do the right thing: apply for placement for the boys. After home inspections and background checks, on October 12, I was approved. The boys had been in the shelter for nine long days.

Upon my arrival, Kasey quickly spotted me. I could hear the stress in his voice when he asked, "Are you here to pick us up?"

"Yes, buddy," I replied as I bent down to hug him. I gathered my great-nephews and all their belongings—only the clothes on their backs—and we went home.

Expecting a call from Sam and Kevin that evening regarding their children, to my astonishment, the phone stayed silent...for three weeks! When Kevin finally did call, I learned he and Sam had been in Stockton. So rather than jumping on board with CPS to get their children back, once they knew the boys were safe with me, they skipped town! I was livid. During that phone conversation, Kevin claimed to not know where Sam was and explained that he was trying to get things in order down there so he could get his boys back. Afraid of being taken advantage of, Matt and I cut to the chase: "Kevin, we're not raising your kids—that's *your* job. Get it together."

"Oh, that won't happen. You won't be raising *my* kids."

Between Kevin's first call and Christmas, he phoned us once or twice a week except during an occasional two-week hiatus which baffled me. I later figured out that he didn't call when he was with Sam. Our discussions were always the same: he was distraught because he didn't know where Sam was; he was trying to get paid by his boss but was getting the runaround; he was trying to get a car. Kasey would ask him about their mother and when he and his brother were going to be picked up. He'd be fed—in a loving tone—a bogus story full of his father's good intentions. Sweet Nick would request a new toy, most often a die-cast "green little mini dirt bike." Kevin would promise to bring him one.

Through the many disappointments dished out by their parents, my great-nephews never lost faith. Being one of the cutest kids on the planet, during mealtimes Nick would remind all of us to pray. At the end of our family prayer, he'd shout, "Amen!" Then he'd giggle. "I opened my eyes while I prayed," or "I was eating while I prayed." Matt and I would be taken aback by his heart of gold, convinced that God doesn't care how you pray if it's legit. Most bedtimes, both Kasey and Nick would pray for protection over their parents and throw in a quick, "And please let our mom and dad pick us up. Amen." Other nights, discouraged from awaiting their parents' return to no avail, the boys maintained their faith but prayed a simple, "Thank you for protecting our mom and dad. Amen."

Kasey and Nick handled the letdowns far better than I did: I wanted to inflict bodily pain on their parents. Beside myself with frustration over Sam and Kevin's lack of action to get back to their children, I looked forward to an evening with my husband... attending Millie's birthday dinner. The adult gathering was held at a pricy steak house, which meant great food and fine wine. It didn't disappoint either. However, nothing was ever easy—or uneventful—when it came to Millie. When the celebration was over and everyone was packing up to leave, Matt's cousin casually joked about her husband, "You know, I was looking around our house yesterday and realized that everything we own—gadgets and whatnot—is Jack's; nothing is mine."

I benignly laughed along. "You know what? Me, too. Matt has a boat, a quad, and his big, black truck; I have a car."

That must have struck a nerve with Millie, because she announced loudly, "But, Jenn, you get the boys!"

Zero to sixty in two seconds flat, my mood thrust from relaxed and jovial to fiery mad. I wanted the boys to have their parents; Millie was well aware of that. She watched and waited for me to hit the ceiling in front of everyone in the public place. Not so much my attitude, but I managed to hold my tongue... somehow. Okay with the fact that we'd likely never have a meaningful relationship, I chose to distance myself from her in the days ahead as much as possible; life was easier that way.

Christmas was approaching, and Kasey was learning carols

for his school's winter program. On the phone one evening, he sat cross-legged under the kitchen table softly singing "Silent Night" to his father. I wished that Kasey's sweet voice could do to Kevin's heart what it was doing to mine—ripping it out. There was still no word from Sam.

Christmas morning, 7:00 a.m. on the dot, the phone rang. It was Kevin. I was surprised by his precise timing; he must have been watching the clock, waiting—like we'd been doing since October! "Hi. Can I talk to the boys?"

Excited for them to receive such a gift, a Christmas wakeup call from their father, I raced to their bedroom and gave them the news: "Morning! Someone wants to talk to you!"

From the receiver, I heard Kevin's loud, happy voice belt out, "Merry Christmas! I love you!" Once the boys realized who was on the phone and what day it was, they were ecstatic.

At last—we made it! Kevin's going to get on board, with or without Sam, and get his children back. Boy, was I wrong.

That call on Christmas morning was the last one Kasey and Nick ever received from their father. In the early part of the next year, 2013, however, their paternal grandmother called to speak to them and told me that Kevin had information on how to reach Sam. Standing within earshot of his mother's side of our conversation, Kevin shouted out a phone number. In that moment I realized he'd known how to get hold of her all along. In a panic, I remembered that I had entrusted Sam with Mom's cremains—given she'd had Lori's. Although Kevin said he didn't know the password, he did know the name of the storage facility where they had put all their belongings—including my sister's ashes—before they were evicted. He said that Mom's cremains were at Lola Platt's house, a family friend from long ago, down in Okieville.

As soon as I got off the phone with Kevin's mother, I tried to reach Sam with the number I'd been given. A man answered. "Hello?"

"Hi, is Sam there?"

"Who is this?" He sounded polite.

"Her aunt. I have her kids."

There was a pause while he went to get her. After a long wait, he came back to the phone: "She said she's not ready to deal with it right now. I tried to get her to talk to you. Can you call back later tonight?"

"Yes," I said. "Thank you."

Next, I contacted the storage facility. The angry manager said that Sam and Kevin indeed had a unit—that they hadn't paid on since they had originally rented it during a one-dollar-down special. She said the past due bill was over eight hundred dollars, but if I gave her the password, she'd allow me access for six. I had no clue what the password was.

As the polite man had suggested, I called again later for Sam and finally got to speak with her...sort of. She kept drifting off in the middle of our conversation. Albeit a brief exchange, Kasey and Nick talked with her, too—which was the first time since I'd picked them up from the emergency shelter. After their how-are-yous, I-miss-yous, and I-love-yous, Sam was so tired that she and the boys said their goodnights. The following evening, I reached out to her again. A bit more attentive, her loving tone with Kasey and Nick, almost like old times, lit them up and gave me a glimmer of hope. That hope evaporated when on day three I called and was told by the polite man, "I'm sorry, Sam's no longer reachable at this number."

Left in the dark—again—two weeks later, I received a second call from Kevin's mom. She asked me to rent a motel room for Sam and her son, who were with her and listening in the background. My initial response was, "Hell no!" but underneath my frustration, I was excited that my niece and her husband were together, as were the boys when I told them. While I considered the request, over her mother-in-law, Sam implored, "Just until Friday, Aunt Jenny, when Kevin gets paid; then we're coming to Oroville to get into a rehab together." That was exactly what I wanted to hear. I confirmed with Sam that was what she and Kevin were going to do, then agreed to rent them a room...for three days. I told her, "I'll give you about a half an hour to get checked in, then I'll call you, and the boys can talk to both of you." Kasey and Nick were ecstatic, as was I; Sam sounded happy, too.

I waited that half hour, then called the room. The telephone was busy. I called again. It was still busy. I called over and over and over. Each time it was busy. I called the motel receptionist. She said the phone was working because Sam had accidentally dialed 911 twice and afterward explained, "It's because of my dyslexia." I knew from the past that was something Sam would say. The receptionist even went to the room for me and gave her a note saying I was trying to call. Still, the phone line remained busy all night long.

Sleep-deprived and mad as ever, at daybreak I called the motel to stop payment on the two subsequent nights I'd agreed to cover. The receptionist said that they were going to kick them out anyway, because Kevin had spent his stay walking around the complex reading loudly out of "a Bible or some sort of book" and disturbing other tenants' rest; some had even checked out because of him.

Once they were booted out of their room, a concerned Sam called wanting to know what was going on. I spelled it out clearly for her: "I'm done. If you two don't want to be parents anymore, I'll find Kasey and Nick new ones!"

I'd unsuspectedly stepped into the CPS case assuming Sam and Kevin would get back on track and in no time get their boys back; never the opposite, that they'd drag things out and straight-up abandon them. The parents had only twelve months "to make substantial progress in alleviating the concerns that led to the initial detention" of their children by CPS. If either or both of them didn't turn things around, I'd be left to rear my great-nephews...except I was done raising kids; it was supposed to be "my turn."

Staying the course, Kasey, Nick, and I pressed on through the slew of physical and emotional ailments the boys had come to me with: eating like they'd never eat again—six scrambled eggs in one sitting for Kasey; multiple bowls of cereal for Nick. Once their appetites leveled off to normal, then they became picky. Anything I made for Kasey wouldn't suffice because, "That's not how my mom used to do it," and Nick would just stare at his plate because, "I don't like it."

Kasey suffered from stomachaches, vomiting, and diarrhea that too many times led to a smelly mishap. At my wit's end, I took him to the doctor who diagnosed him with encopresis. She said it had been caused by his chronic constipation, that I was unaware of, which was likely a result of not eating a proper diet and—what else?—stress. Luckily, for poor Kasey's sake—and mine!—a regimen of no dairy products, MiraLAX stool softener twice a day, and restroom reminders alleviated his symptoms.

Emotions usually ran high for the now six-year-old, too, because he often felt victimized by other children and slighted by adults. Each evening when I picked him up from school, he'd have a meltdown in the car, and it was always for the same reason: he'd been mistreated by a student, "And the teacher got *me* in trouble instead of *him!*" Contrary to Kasey's perception of the teachers, they looked out for him, thank goodness, as one afternoon he nearly hopped onto a bus full of high schoolers—and he didn't ride a bus.

Nick feared people in general, and abandonment. He and I passed on several excellent daycare providers because, no matter what accommodations were made, he just didn't feel safe at any of them without me. The first few times when the YMCA was my only option, the staff had to peel him—screaming at the top of his lungs—off me so I could get to work on time.

Kasey's meltdowns and Nick's fits of terror continued until, when all else failed, I stooped to bribery. "Kasey, if you'll do your best to get along with the other students during the school week, come Friday I'll buy you a new toy." And, "Nick, if you can just try to be brave when I drop you at daycare, you'll get one, too." It was the only thing that worked. In time, Kasey's emotional upsets became less frequent; and at my departure from Nick's daycare, he'd nervously verify, "Are you going to pick me up?" Once I reassured him that, yes, I would, the uncertainty that filled his big, brown eyes vanished and he'd go about his day.

Anytime the power went out, it was a disaster of apocalyptic proportions. When an evening storm brought an electrical outage to our neighborhood, distraught Kasey and Nick hightailed it across the living room floor and buried their faces in my side. They remained there even after Matt located the flashlights and lit the kerosene lamps and candles. It wasn't until after he dug out the generator and fired it up to turn the interior lights back on that the boys finally calmed down, sort of. Uncle Matt was their hero that evening. Then, one morning I was getting ready for work and blew a fuse with my hairdryer. We could see just fine, but Kasey and Nick once again panicked and buried their heads in my side. Then and there I knew something was amiss; it wasn't just the darkness they were afraid of when the electricity went out.

Bewildered by my great-nephews' disabling fear of power outages, it wasn't until Kasey opened up to me that I understood. While he was brushing his perfect, blond curls flat and to the side—just like he preferred—he conveyed, "Aunt Jenny, I can tell you how we got here, I just don't know why. First, they came and took our truck. Then the electricity was turned off because my parents didn't pay the bill. Then the landlord came and kicked us out, but we'd sneak in at night through a screen door. We'd cook our food on a little grill outside. Then we stayed at all kinds of motels. Then we stayed at cousins' houses. Then I woke up in a shopping cart with groceries in it in the bathroom of a park."

My heart sank.

The boys' nighttime struggles far outweighed their daytime ones. Before bed, I had to secure their room, every single evening. Kasey would demand, "Aunt Jenny, I want the door closed." Nick would argue, "But I want it open." If they wouldn't compromise, I'd set it firmly in the middle. Their blinds had to be completely shut; not one iota of visibility anywhere. Lastly, they needed their special stuffed animal or toy of the night and my promise to leave their television on—static-screen muted, it didn't matter—while they slept. If I didn't keep my promise, they'd wake right back up as I learned the hard way. Convincing them to swap the illumination of their TV for that of night-lights—one in every outlet of their room—was nothing short of intervention on my part.

Each night, after my great-nephews' bedroom was secure, the three of us would crowd on the bottom bunk. The good forty-five minutes to an hour before they'd fall asleep was our time to snuggle, read books, sing songs, and simply chat about whatever was on their busy minds, which was a lot. Nick, without fail, would remind me how much he missed his parents, and one evening explained why he and his brother had yet to be picked up: "Aunt Jenny, my dad's taking so long because he's working hard so he can buy us a castle." Left speechless, I wished that was the case. Just before Nick would drift off into slumber, he'd murmur, "Aunt Jenny, you're beautiful...I love you." Then, searching for some semblance of his mother, the once breastfed child would try to inch his hand down my shirt. I'd stop him midway and whisper, "No, Brother, no ninny there." When Kasey was good and tired, he'd climb up top where sometimes I'd hear him grumble, "I wonder when my mom and dad are going to pick us up." Other times, he'd softly cry himself to sleep.

On a good night, once Kasey and Nick were slumbering peacefully, I'd enjoy the comfort of my own bed until the alarm went off in the early morning. However, that rarely happened. Nick hated to sleep alone, and anytime he woke up without me in his bed, he'd do whatever it took to get me back into it. Some nights, two or three times even, he'd slink through my room to where I was sleeping and whisper, "Aunt Jenny, I'm scared" or "Aunt Jenny, I have to pee" or "Aunt Jenny, I had a bad dream." Half asleep, I'd follow him back to his bed, where I'd stay until dawn.

At four o'clock one morning, Nick was sneaking into my room when Matt's cell phone alarm went off. Flailing and screaming, he swept across my bedroom floor straight into my solid wood bed post. It happened so quickly there was nothing I could do. According to Nick after the fact, Matt's (elk ringtone) alarm sounded exactly like a zombie. *Really?* When his preschool teacher asked him how he'd gotten the red, raised egg that was front and center on his forehead, embarrassed, he replied, "It's a secret."

Nick had occasional nightmares, and many of them involved zombies. One of his scariest was of a zombie eating his mother's brains! He couldn't stop crying.

One sleepless evening, I asked both Kasey and Nick, "What are you afraid of?"

In unison they chimed, "Zombies!"

Zombies...of course. Putting two and two together, it made perfect sense—the boys' angst over the bedroom door being closed versus open, the blinds having to be completely shut, and the static-screen TV on all night—my great-nephews' paranoia stemmed from that of tweakers, not zombies. Boy did I want to elaborate on the striking similarities between the two types of walking dead, but instead, I reassured them, "Kasey, Nick, we're upstairs, not on the ground floor. Plus, we have Dottie Mae, who is super protective. There's no way any zombies, if they were real that is, would ever get to us. Besides, Uncle Matt hunts, so he has guns. He'd kill those zombies before they ever came near our property."

Nick asked, "Uncle Matt has guns?"

"Yes, buddy."

"Oh."

With nothing more to say, Kasey and Nick peacefully drifted off to sleep.

The next day was a trip for a new toy. Kasey knew exactly what he wanted from the store and grabbed a Skylander character to add to his collection. Nick, on the other hand, was undecided and took his sweet time choosing. Usually he ran straight to the "little mini dirt bike" section, but not this time. Nope. He combed through aisle after aisle of toys. After what seemed like an eternity, he handed me a package containing a sheriff's badge, a rifle, and a handgun with a holster. I didn't think much of it except, *Geez...finally*.

That night at bedtime, Nick asked, "Aunt Jenny, can I wear my gun to bed?"

"Sure."

Over pajamas, he slowly and methodically put on his holster, placed his toy handgun in it, grabbed his rifle, and sat on the bed. As he lay down, he arranged the rifle on top of the blanket and across his chest. In his most sincere tone, he declared, "Aunt Jenny, I'm done with those skeleton zombies." Kasey and I couldn't help but titter at his seriousness; nevertheless, we all slept well for the next several nights.

When Nick's arsenal of weapons no longer made him feel safe from zombies, I searched my mind for something else that could kill them. *Wait. A zombie is already dead.* I asked, "Nick, what can beat up zombies?"

"The Hulk!" he exclaimed.

"You know what? You're right!" I went further, "Do you know that Uncle Matt *loves* the Hulk? That's his favorite character. In fact, very few people know this, but Uncle Matt *is* the Hulk. I've only seen it a couple of times, but if anyone—I mean anyone—messes with his family, and you're his family, it makes him so angry that he starts turning green and he gets really beefed up and his clothes start tearing right off his body. Yep. *Nobody* wants to mess with Uncle Matt's family."

Nick accepted my fib as though he'd heard it during a Sunday morning service, still his inability to sleep persisted for months.

Kasey had a tough time sleeping through the night as well. Sometimes, wondering where he was, he'd call out for me; other times, I'd overhear him having a night terror, which is like a nightmare, only freakier. As if to ensure that I'd suffer from sleep deprivation, the night terrors most often occurred right *after* I dozed off—and the first one I witnessed nearly scared the bejesus out of me.

Awakened to Kasey yelling at someone—or something—I ran into his room and found him sitting upright on his bed. "Kasey, it's okay. It's Aunt Jenny. I'm right here," I softly tried to talk him through it.

"Oh," he uttered, "*it's* right by you."

"What? What's right by me, Kasey?" I did an immediate one-eighty and scanned the room under the soft illumination of the nightlights.

Then, as if *The Exorcist* met *The Amityville Horror*, he tells *it*, "Get out!"

I turned back around and faced Kasey, who was still sitting upright. My voice dropped, "Boy, I'm glad you didn't just say that to me."

Whatever *it* was, it must have left, because Kasey settled back under the covers. I returned to my bed, where I lay wide awake for the rest of the night.

During another of his terrors, I awoke to a ruckus in Nick's and his room. Engaged in a one-person tussle on the floor, Kasey was frantically screaming, "I'm losing! I'm losing!" I had no choice but to wake him. When he (sort of) came to, he said he was dreaming he was inside a video game, fighting for his life, and having fallen from a bridge, he was plummeting into a bottomless pit. As with the others, come morning, he had no recollection of that night terror; it was so odd.

In time, Kasey's scary episodes lessened in frequency and intensity, and they became more like the night I awoke to him repeatedly calling my name. "Aunt Jenny. Aunt Jenny. Aunt Jenny."

Staggering from a deep sleep, I approached his top bunk.

Unaware that he was dreaming, I asked, "Yes, Kasey? What do you need?"

Sitting upright in his bed again, and looking at and speaking directly to me, he said, "I can't find my Aunt Jenny."

Realizing he was fast asleep, I whispered, "I am right here, Kasey." As if lost, he gazed at me in confusion. All it took that time to get him to lay back down was a quick prayer for peaceful rest.

The difficult nights made for terrible days. Matt was my support through it all. Most mornings I'd find a love note from him written on a paper napkin, towel, or even plate next to my coffee cup and spoon. With java in hand and caffeine in system, I'd place the note atop the growing stack on my dresser, then seize the day—or try. More times than not, I was a dead-tired zombie at work, often arriving with pink children's Amoxicillin splotches on one sleeve of my jacket and pink Pepto-Bismol (for myself) on the other.

———

Sam would eventually want to get back on track and call me—I believed that, I just hoped she didn't wait until it was too late for her to reunite with her sons. In case she didn't come through, and it was leaning that way, I needed a backup plan. Deep down I knew I couldn't keep Kasey and Nick—it was supposed to be my turn—yet I didn't know if I could let them go to somebody else either. Then it occurred to me that when they returned to the States from the U.K., Penny and Stewart had adopted not one but two sons. It was the scariest email I ever sent, but in it I asked Penny if she knew anyone who might be interested in adopting my great-nephews; I knew I could trust my sister's judgment. She replied she would ask around.

For a drug called "speed," it sure makes people go slow. Kasey and Nick had not heard from Kevin since Christmas morning—in over three months!—and Sam (except for the two brief phone calls) in five. On March 8, to be exact, the phone rang: "Aunt Jenny, everybody keeps telling me to go take care of my boys, I'm going to lose them, and they're going to be adopted out. I'm tired of hearing it. Will you please help me? Please, please, please, please, please..." She was in Stockton, at Lola's.

Knowing that five of the twelve months allowed by CPS for Sam to reunite with her boys had passed, and sensing she wasn't wholeheartedly committed to stepping up, I said, "I think it's too late," then added, "but if you're serious, call me at eight tomorrow morning, and I'll drive down and pick you up." I stressed to her that, because of the lost time, it was important she follow through with everything CPS asked.

"Oh, I will. I promise. Thank you, Aunt Jenny. Thank you. Thank you."

I didn't think she'd call, but she did—at eight o'clock sharp! I grabbed my purse and made the two-hour drive to Stockton—more specifically, Okieville.

When I rolled into town, and down Memory Lane, I parked in front of Lola's house and phoned Sam to let her know I was outside. Sam wasn't there, however; she was down the road. Lola brought out Mom's urn, for which I thanked her, and Sam's bags. She said that Sam would be right back. I waited...and waited. A strung-out-on-drugs woman on a bicycle, somehow aware I was there for Sam, rode up alongside my car and offered to show me where she was. Afraid I might get robbed, or worse—I was in Okieville after all—I politely declined. When I was just about ready to say 'Forget it' and go home, I saw Sam in my rear-view mirror. Moseying in my direction, it didn't appear she was in much of a hurry. When she arrived at my car, we loaded her duffle bag into the back and headed north. Oh, the irony of driving through Okieville with my mom in the backseat: thirty-five years earlier, it had been the exact opposite.

On the way to Oroville, more than thankful Sam had finally called me, I began updating her on Kasey and Nick. She was happy to hear how well they were doing in school and otherwise. I didn't bother to rattle her about the ailments they were still struggling with; I was hopeful they would be something of the past. But when I showed her pictures of the boys on my cell phone, she quickly glanced at them and gave an "Aw," like they were someone else's kids.

Wow.

I changed the subject. "Did you really have a gastric bypass, or did you just say that because you lost so much weight from doing drugs?" That was a question I really wanted answered.

Unwavering, she responded, "Kevin and I both had a bypass. See?" She lifted her shirt to show me the three puncture scars on her stomach.

Just in case we lost touch again, I made sure to get the password for the storage unit where her mom's cremains were kept so I could contact the facility later.

I had no idea where to start in getting drug treatment for Sam. First, though, she needed to deal with that warrant and her two failures to appear at court by turning herself in at the jail. Reluctantly, she agreed...until we got closer to town that is. Then she decided she would rather go to the hospital. I told her no. We pulled into the jail parking lot, and I walked her all the way in to be sure she didn't change her mind. It was a successful turn-in, but due to overcrowding, she was booted out within two hours. So much for drying her out and getting her into a court-ordered residential drug treatment program right away! Per CPS, she couldn't stay with me because I had her boys. Sam's sister Stephanie graciously allowed her to move in with her—so long as she stayed clean—until she could get into a rehab. Unfortunately, in our area, the free rehabs were full and the others were expensive.

The very day after I picked up Sam, March 9, Kevin called my house looking for his wife. He didn't bother to ask about his boys. In fact, he hadn't called or spoken to them since Christmas morning. Obviously, they were no longer his concern...but they were still mine. I felt he wanted to sabotage Sam's reunion with Kasey and Nick, and it was clear that he didn't have her best interests in mind, so I belted into the phone's receiver, "Don't ever call my home again!" and hung up.

Since I now had the password to the storage unit that Kevin and Sam said held my sister Lori's ashes, I picked the phone back up and contacted the facility's manager. Hoping she'd let me in to get the urn—if it was really there—without paying the excessive back fees that would have been a hardship for me, I gave her the secret code. Instead, she told me that she'd have to speak with "corporate" about the situation and to call back the next day. When I did, I was told, "I'm sorry, I still haven't heard from corporate; can you give me a week or so, then check in again?" I did that many times, until I was told by some man, "If you don't stop harassing our business, I'm going to call the police on you." Apparently, there really was no "corporate."

Sam immediately took the steps prescribed by CPS and started visiting Kasey and Nick. I was there when she saw them for the first time—after five months! I could see a glimpse of the proud, proud mother she used to be. I knew how much she loved them, although it had been hidden under her addiction. She looked the boys up and down, eying the outfits they were wearing, then grumbled to me through Kasey, "You need new shoes." A new pair of shoes was the least of my worries, but that was Sam: always fixated on appearances. All the same, she was visiting her sons regularly and, as far as I knew, doing everything she should.

Trying to be as supportive as possible, yet careful to not be taken advantage of, I spent a full day driving Sam around town helping her get her affairs in order. Since she'd lost all her identification, we visited the DMV for a new California I.D; and since she needed a job, we went to the Salvation Army for some clothes she could look for work in. While shopping, thinking she could kill two birds with one stone, Sam sought out the manager to ask for a job application. The manager, who just happened to be holding one in her hand, looked down at Sam and said, "I'm sorry, this is the only one I have." That was disappointing; the Salvation Army was supposed to stand for so much more than arrogant liars. I paid for Sam's items, then we stormed out.

Sam and I were scoping out places where she could seek employment when we drove past Little Caesar's Pizza. One of their employees, looking as jubilant as ever, was dancing on the corner waving a sign that announced, "$5 pizzas!"

"Sam," I asked, "wouldn't it be cool if you got a job there, and I drove up next to you with the boys in the car? They'd see you working hard for them!" I imagined it so perfectly.

Sam laughed, "I know, right?" but I could tell that wasn't quite her vision.

We stopped at Wal-Mart. Sam had nearly completed her job application via the kiosk when all the information she had inputted disappeared. Infuriated, she stood up and—like she was a member of Wal-Mart's Walton family or something—demanded, "I need to speak to a manager!" A split second later, she gave me a somewhat startled look, like *Oh, shit, I'm on the bottom of the food chain now.* She sat back down, and quietly redid her app.

Before dropping Sam at her sister Stephanie's house, I stopped at different apartment complexes and she picked up rental applications. If she did find a job, my hope was that she could get into a place and, under a social worker's supervision, have her boys back in her care.

Unfortunately, beating addiction isn't a cakewalk, and Sam began to struggle with hers. In a phone conversation, Stephanie cried, "Aunt Jenny, I want to help my sister, but I think she's still using. She comes and goes at all hours of the night and leaves food and dirty dishes all over the house. I told her to clean up after herself, and she got so hostile that we almost got into a physical fight! I don't want this around my daughter. I'm sorry, but she has to go." Thereafter, in a downward spiral, Sam stayed at place after place—because the homeowners kept kicking her out—all while she insisted to everyone she was "doing great."

Matt and I had planned to spend our eleventh anniversary in Maui. Yes, *the* beautiful Maui. Reservations for our flights, accommodations, and even excursions had been in place long before I picked Kasey and Nick up from the emergency shelter. I refused to forgo our—especially my—much needed getaway, so rather than cancel our trip, to make it up to Kasey and Nick, I promised them three days in Disneyland beforehand.

Child Protective Services wouldn't allow it, but I wanted Sam to accompany the boys and me to "The Happiest Place on Earth"—it would have been good for her, too—then watch them, under the supervision of a social worker of course, in my home while I was away in Maui. I didn't argue too much about Sam not being permitted to visit Disneyland with us, but I did assert my position, with tact, that she should watch the boys the long week I'd be gone. "I can barely find Kasey and Nick a sitter for one day, let alone seven straight," and, "A stranger through CPS respite watching them isn't going to cut it—the boys will be traumatized all over again!" I told the social worker.

While pressing CPS to allow Sam more time with Kasey and Nick—at Disneyland and in my own home—I was knocked sideways by my niece's downward spiral. Via a telephone call, she wept, "Aunt Jenny, I don't know what to do. Everybody keeps kicking me out of places. I am not doing anything to these people. I sit in my room all day and leave them alone. I am not the loud, rude little girl I used to be. It is not me this time. It's them.

It is the same as it was in Stockton, except there I was high. I can't even take care of myself. Just find a home for my boys."

I could hardly breathe.

Just two weeks before Matt's and my anniversary vacation, I kept my promise to Kasey and Nick and took them to Disneyland. We flew from Sacramento to Long Beach Airport, hopped onto the Super Shuttle to the Pier Hotel, and then made a dash to the park. Three days of rides, cotton candy, and Mickey Mouse hats gave us a nice distraction from our circumstances...for the most part. On our last night at "The Happiest Place on Earth," we were watching fireworks from our hotel window when Nick yelled, "Oh, a shooting star!" He then closed his eyes and said, "I wish my mom and dad would pick us up."

At the Long Beach Airport, waiting to board the plane to go home, Nick sat patiently listening to music via headphones. Singing Fun's "We Are Young," he'd mumble the words he didn't know, then burst out with, "Tonight...we are young...so let's set the world on fire...we can burn brighter than the sun...." Our fellow passengers thought he was the cutest kid, as did I. Kasey, on the other hand, had something up his sleeve—I mean under his hat. Just as we were about to board the plane, I couldn't find my driver's license. People were loading up, and I was in a panic retracing my steps from the bathroom to the snack shop and back to the waiting area. As the last on-boarder passed through, Kasey pulled my license out from underneath his cap. He thought it was quite hysterical; I wasn't amused in the slightest.

When we returned from Disneyland, I still had no one to keep Kasey and Nick while I'd be away in Maui—and I'd sorted through my, albeit short, list of family members and friends who might be available many times over. At the eleventh hour, my nephew Stanley and his wife agreed to take them. Matt and I caught our direct flight out of Sacramento to Kahului.

Our seven days in Hawaii—maybe "The *Second* Happiest Place on Earth"—were well spent. Matt and I waited above the clouds to witness a Haleakala (10,000 feet elevation) sunrise and unwound on the beaches under magnificent sunsets. We snorkeled at the Molokini Crater and trekked along Black Sand Beach and other gems hidden along Hana Highway. We explored the lush green Iao Valley and visited the Maui Ocean Center. We meandered through the Banyan Tree Park and, during a dinner cruise, relished the view of a grand rainbow over Lahaina. We felt the rush of the Nakalele Blowhole and got our fill of food and entertainment at the Honua'ula Luau. Our previous Fort Bragg trip times a hundred, Maui didn't disappoint.

My return from heaven felt like hell—Sam's "just find a home for my boys" was more of a reality than ever. Contact with her was hit and miss, she often skipped visits, and she stopped her case plan with CPS. It wasn't likely that Kasey and Nick were going to be reunited with their mother, and my adopting them wasn't a possibility. The hard truth was, if they went to the wrong person, I could lose them forever. I was falling apart. With impeccable timing, Penny emailed to tell me a friend she had approached about adopting the boys, if things didn't work out with Sam, was interested. That friend was Marie.

As soon as I could, I obtained permission from the Court to fly my great-nephews out to Colorado, where Marie lived. I wanted them to meet each other—discretely, of course—so I could decide if this was the best adoptive placement. Since Penny and Marie lived in the same town, I simply told Kasey and Nick we were going to visit my sister. We did visit my sister—but also her friend Marie—so it wasn't a full-fledged lie.

Marie fell head over heels for the boys, and they, although unaware of who she was or might become, seemed drawn to her as well. She fed, bathed, and got them ready for bed. Enjoying the break, I was like...*yes!*

Marie, confident that she wanted to pursue adoption of my great-nephews, as that looked to be where they were heading, privately asked me, "What is this going to look like?"

Clueless, I answered, "I don't know. I'm going to leave it to the professionals who do it all the time."

With a backup plan now in place for the boys, I returned to California full of hope and a whole lot lighter—from the weight that had been lifted off my shoulders. However, as was the pattern in my life, that hope turned to gloom when, several weeks later, I received an email from Marie. It said, "I'm sorry to have to send you this, Jenn, I know it's not what you want to hear. I've rigorously weighed with family and friends and the professionals I know the pros and cons of being an adoptive parent to Kasey and Nick, and I'm sorry, but I don't think it's in the boys' best interest to be raised by me, a single mom."

It was obvious Marie was simply doing what she felt was best for my great-nephews. Still, I was crushed.

Back to square one, I continued in my endeavors to find a home for Kasey and Nick. Along the way, I met different people and their—often, adopted—children. When I met the little blond girl with a flower in her hair whose name I recognized from the confidential CPS courtroom, I felt like I'd regained consciousness after being sucker-punched: I may not lose my beloved family members through this process of adopting "out" after all; depending how I looked at it, I may actually acquire beloved family members through this process of adopting "in." However, no matter where Kasey and Nick landed, I knew following through with it was going to be rough.

CHAPTER THIRTEEN

THE VAULT

*"To Jennie-fer, I will always love you
no matter what..."*

I t was July of 2013, nine months after Kasey and Nick had been abandoned by their parents, and they were still awaiting an adoptive home. Matt and I were in the kitchen trying to figure out what to cook for dinner while the boys were starting on their homework. As always, the TV was too loud; and Dottie Mae was barking, this time because a car had pulled into our driveway. We all looked out the sliding glass door to see who it was, then Matt and I made eye contact. *What the hell is going on?*

Sitting in the driver's seat was my sixty-eight-year-old father who suffered from alcohol-induced dementia. He'd managed to travel 150 miles to our house. I was surprised that he had found us, since we now lived in the mountains, and asked him how he did it. He said he got our address off the Father's Day card I had sent him the month before and, once in Oroville, stopped at an AM/PM gas station to ask for directions. The clerk there printed a Google map for him.

Dad stepped out of his car with his small dog Misty and showed me a human bite on his forearm. He said Pat, my stepmom, had him arrested for a new domestic violence charge. Having bailed himself out of jail, he was sitting at home when the sheriff arrived with a restraining order telling him to vacate the premises. He explained, "I had nowhere else to go."

After nearly thirty years of marriage, Pat was divorcing my father—and he ended up at my door. On top of trying to meet my great-nephews' needs, I spent the next months trying to make sense of Dad's medical, financial, and legal issues: Medicare, his Social Security and pension income, the divorce, and new criminal charge. I knew he needed an attorney, so that's where I started. First things first, the lawyer drafted a Durable Power of Attorney for me over my dad, as well as a will. As he was inputting information, Dad had to recite his children's names, dates of birth, etc., who were "conceived within the marriage of" such and such. When it came to me, the youngest, I popped in, "Dad wasn't married to my mom or named on my birth certificate, but there was a DNA test done to confirm I was his."

The attorney responded, "That's good that you said that; otherwise, you would have been left out. We'll have to reword it. While typing, he spoke under his breath, "Conceived to Ivan Wade and Barbara Seifert. There." Then he looked at me with a grin and said, "You're a love child."

I heard him, but I asked, "I'm sorry, what?"

He explained, "You don't hear the term much anymore, but a child born out of wedlock used to be commonly referred to as a 'love child.'"

A bit irritated at the irony, I replied, "Oh. So that's what you call it. I'm a love child." *I've always called it something else: fucked.*

After completing the Power of Attorney and will, we retained the lawyer to handle Dad's divorce and new domestic violence matter, too. With legal representation in place, all we had to do was wait for the settlement conferences and court dates—sort of the same situation as Kasey and Nick's.

Dad's timing to show up at my door couldn't have been worse, but it gave me an opportunity to pick his brain about the past to try to put some pieces into the puzzle, like whether it was he who told Mom to call a cab at my birth and/or cut her nightgowns off.

"Dad, were you and Mom together when I was born?"

"No. I was in jail. I did six months for two pills: reds. I didn't like pot, I just sold it to make two bucks a bag. Your mother liked pot and pills; I only liked pills."

Too much information, Dad. My blood began to boil, but I kept my cool.

"Your mom got pregnant with you so she'd have something to remember me by."

"Oh, right. Do you remember Willy?"

"No. I only remember her husband Stan. She was still married to him when we were together."

"Well, when she went into labor with me, whoever she was with told her to call a cab. That wasn't you?"

"No. I was in jail."

"And you never came home and cut her nightgowns off her?"
With a pause, "No."

"Oh. Okay. Well, she married Stan, Philip, Junior, and then
Billy Jack. You don't remember Philip either?"

"No. Damn, how many times has your mother been married?
Four? Five times?"

"I thought five, but I can only count four. I don't know if I'm
leaving someone out."

"Damn."

Annoyed by his arrogance, in a tone of voice filled with sar-
casm, I spouted: "But, Dad, you're on your third divorce."

"Oh, yeah."

I ended our conversation by walking away.

Stress had caused hives to develop all over Dad's back, and
his skin became infected. While seeking medical attention for
him, I asked his doctor, who happened to be Asian, about outside resources to help me care for him. The doctor explained, as
if I were a bad person for asking such a thing, "In my culture, we
would have family members, relatives, to take care of our parents; that's not like in your culture."

*Dad spent his entire life thinking only about himself—not me, Pen-
ny, or Debbie. He did nothing to make sure our needs were met, yet he
raised his soon-to-be ex-wife's children. Where are they now? Mr. Medical Doctor, I'm sure your parents did their part in taking care of you.*

Later that night, still irked about the doctor's comment, I
vented to Matt: "It is really just not fair that I get stuck doing
this. Pat and Dad built a life together. Dad gets sick, and she

boots him out. They took care of her kids—one gets all the cars and one gets the house. Must be nice! Why aren't her kids here taking care of him? The hundred dollars a month child support didn't cut it on my end. Do you know how hard it is to find Mother's and Father's Day cards for parents like mine? The cards have to be humorous, because neither of them did what they were supposed to do. I'm tired of taking care of people. *Who took care of me?!"*

Matt searched his heart for a comforting answer to my question, then replied, "Ever since I've known you, you have always had that picture of the beach on your bathroom wall that reads: "When you see only one set of footprints..."

I knew the rest: *...it was then that I carried you.* Matt was right, except rather than travel through the sand, I wanted to stop and bury my head in it and come out again when the coast was clear. Unfortunately, that wasn't an option; for my great-nephews' and now Dad's sake, I had to see things through, somehow.

In fight-or-flight mode—with nowhere to flee—the next evening I asked Matt for some privacy, which he agreed to give me, and I picked up a pencil and paper. I had no idea how to write a memoir, but that night *Smoke Ring Rising* was conceived. Once that first word went down, "Post-It" notes hidden deep in my memory flowed out like a spigot full force that wouldn't shut off. I couldn't jot down the happy stories fast enough; the sad ones took days, sometimes weeks, to pen, notwithstanding the fact I had little to no time to myself.

Somewhere in the middle of my first draft, I cried to Matt: "I can't do it. I can't do it. Some of my memories are just too painful to think about, let alone write about. It really hurts."

His advice: "Maybe you could put it down for a while and come back to it later. It *is* consuming you."

I wanted to put it down for good. "Do you think I should keep writing?"

"I think you should...didn't you tell me you made a promise to God once, something about you'll always give?"

Still in tears, "I forgot about that. I did."

"You don't know who you're going to help. It may be our own kids."

"Matt, does my past embarrass you?"

He paused, then shook his head no. "You were just a kid. Besides, who did you have to look up to?"

My husband was mostly right: I was just a kid, and who *did* I have to look up to? But here's where he was wrong: that reasoning applied to everyone *but* me because I believed I was exempt from being pardoned.

The more I wrote, the more I felt my story, in the end, would be nothing more than a train wreck as witnessed from the inside out, but I continued anyway. The writing part somehow gave me relief; the delving-into-the-past part, not so much.

Accompanied by a glass of wine, late one evening I lifted the lid off the storage tote that held, simply put, my history. Resting on top were bags that contained photos I'd separated by era—Rick, then Bert—that never made it into albums. Underneath the bags lay various keepsakes I'd saved: academic awards my children and I had received, a published article written by my niece Stephanie, and a newspaper clipping of when my nephew

Steven pitched an entire Little League baseball game, striking out eleven batters and allowing only five hits and five runs. The stack of accomplishments made me smile.

Further inside the container, I found a neatly folded piece of paper. On the outside, in Sam's handwriting, it said, "Only my Aunt Jenny is worthy of opening this." Inside, she thanked me for taking care of her when her mother, Lori, died. My eyes filled with tears; *I no longer feel worthy of opening this.*

A strip from a fortune cookie I'd received years earlier caught my attention. My life in ten words: "The finest of structures can house the worst of evil." I laughed. *If I had only been taught that in grammar school!*

Waiting at the bottom for me was the "vault," that shoebox of photos I'd been the keeper of since childhood. It held picture after picture of my people; the majority of whom were no longer alive.

In black and white film, as if they had a part in a Humphrey Bogart movie, Grandma Maggie and Grandpa Wayne stood next to a fireplace. Grandpa wore his Fedora, cocked to the side; a tobacco pipe hung from his mouth. Grandma wore her long coat, a scarf over her head, and held a cigarette between her index and middle finger. I paused. *Still the Greatest Generation.*

Another was a portrait of Mom sporting a blond beehive while holding Teresa and Lori, who must have been only two and one. Neither Brian nor I had been born yet. *My mother the 1960s suburban housewife type—and a blonde to boot! Unbelievable.*

Mom, a few years later, in 1969. Smiling, she was seated comfortably on a couch with her feet on the coffee table; her high heels tossed underneath. Wearing a blue button-up dress, I could see the slip peeking out from underneath. *Mom never wore dresses or heels, let alone a slip. Hell, she hated underwear.* I still hadn't been born, but my siblings were standing arm-in-arm next to a Christmas tree. Dressed for the holiday, Teresa and Lori wore white dresses with polka dots and a large red bow; Brian had on slacks and a striped dress shirt. *Wow...my blond-haired, blue-eyed hellion sisters look so innocent.*

Pictures of me as a newborn and infant didn't exist, which used to make me feel somewhat invisible, but I had come to terms with it. According to the handful of photos I had, I arrived into the world at age two. At least that's the earliest photo of myself I've ever seen. A two-year-old, I'm in blond braids, wearing blue and white Oshkosh B'gosh overalls, and holding a red ball. I peered long and hard at the professional portrait. *I look happy...well taken care of. I sure don't feel that way now.* In another, about age three, I'm at Grandma and Grandpa's. It's Christmastime, and my siblings and I are opening presents. *Wrapping paper everywhere! Good times.* Two more, at approximately four, I'm playing in the backyard at my grandparents' home. *My happy place; I long for it so.* Missing from the vault was a photo taken inside Farrell's Ice Cream Parlour in Eugene, Oregon. Celebrating my fifth birthday with Mom, her husband Philip, and his side of the family, I was wearing a dress—like always—and standing on the table enjoying the day. *Where did my picture go? Shoot!* One I needed to add to the vault used to hang on the wall of Dad's home, the one he'd been restrained from. *I'd better not forget to get it from Pat.*

More images of my sisters; they were older, but still living at our grandparents' home. Lori, about eleven, is sitting in the yard on a wooden flatbed wagon, likely built by Grandpa; Teresa, about twelve, barefoot and in bell-bottoms, is standing out front in the street.

Another of Lori, now sixteen. Pregnant with Sam, she's dressed as a pumpkin for Halloween.

At the bottom of the vault were photos of Jonny. *Huh? Well, he is family.* In one, he's at my trailer in Concow, seated in a recliner. Wearing Levi's and his black riding jacket, he'd ridden his motorcycle up from Oroville to visit me. Nostalgia hit: *This is the one of him I took by ambush...and captured his perfect smile. That was a lovely day; a happy time for us—before everything changed.* Another was the one he gave me when we reconnected after Lori's funeral. Seated next to his daughter, he's beaming like a proud father should. In the last, a 2x3 wallet-size, he is attired in a brown, collared dress shirt. *I don't recall receiving this one at all.* I scrutinized it closely. *Something is off with him here. His smile isn't genuine, or warm.* I flipped it over and read the back: "Senior, 1987. To Jennie-fer, I will always love you no matter what. Love, Jonny." *Oh, his twelfth-grade year—the year we parted ways. No wonder I don't recall it.* I reread it, then said aloud, "You'll always love me no matter what!" The nostalgia I'd felt passed, and every unsettled emotion within my core came surging back to the surface. *Is it me, or meth? Jonny, you left me all alone. I wanted to spend my life with you, but YOU abandoned me! Might as well have left me for dead!* I wanted to scream, but instead shoved my history back into the vault and put it away. For several minutes, my heart pounded like it had been excised from my chest and was gasping for blood. I sat on the floor, confused. *This...must be how Kasey and Nick feel.* I thought about Tim saying a drink or two once or twice a week is fine, but I killed a bottle of wine that night. After, I made my way to bed, figured I'd try to deal with life some other time.

When morning came, I continued my probe into the past, but via the Internet. On Ancestry.com, I found Mom right away. Her first marriage to pop up was in 1973 to Jessie Willard Witt, aka, Willy. *I was right; she did marry five times!* I had his full name and birthdate now, so I Googled him. *Oh, my.* I found newspaper article after newspaper article.

The first: 1959, a disturbance case. "Jessie Willard Witt, age 19, was arrested for using loud and profane language in front of the complainant's home, brandishing a knife, and public drunkenness while awaiting trial on charges of battery, peace disturbance, and malicious mischief." *So Willy—not Ivan—was the "Jenny's dad" who liked to play with knives...cut nightgowns off women. That's good news.*

1982, "Jessie Willard Witt, age 43, was arraigned on narcotics and weapons charges; possession of a controlled substance for sale, possession of narcotics paraphernalia, being a convicted felon in possession of a handgun, carrying a concealed weapon, and carrying a loaded weapon. Witt, who was allegedly carrying a small case and a leather coat over his arm, ran from an officer. Along the way, Witt allegedly dropped the case with seven balloons containing a substance believed to be heroin and a .22 caliber handgun." *Heroin...wow. A leather jacket? Ha! I knew it was his coat I ruined while sleeping on it with bubblegum in my mouth!*

In 1983, "A 43-year-old man, Jessie Willard Witt, was arrested on a felony charge of child molestation. Investigators believe Witt molested a three-year-old female while he was out on a day pass from the County Honor Farm." *A three-year-old? Wait. In 1973, when he and Mom got married, I would have been two, or close to it...Lori, eight. Eight—the age she told me she'd been molested.* It was everything I could do to not vomit.

2008. The last article I found was an obituary for Jessie "Papa" Witt. In it was a black and white picture of a man in a cowboy hat—the same man I once had a picture of standing next to a bridge, holding a can of beer. It read: "He enjoyed being a father, grandfather, and spending time with his grandchildren. His hobbies included fishing and whittling." *Huh? Mom used to say, "Jenny used to sit and whittle with her dad." Sick bastard.*

The "I'll always love you no matter what" from Jonny I'd found in the vault and the alarming articles about Willy I'd found online sent my emotions into a tailspin. *Love is forgiving as well as for giving...but damn.*

CHAPTER FOURTEEN

LOVE IS THICKER THAN BLOOD

I hoped they would get settled into a family that would accept me, too, as I was the closest thing to their grandma and their history...

K asey and Nick's court matters dragged on, and I had no idea what the outcome would be. I didn't want to chance my great-nephews getting bounced around from foster home to foster home or, even worse, separated during the process, so during one of our telephone conversations, I told the social worker that I wanted them with me until she located a solid pre-adoptive home. That way, if Sam progressed and got them back somehow, great; if she didn't, then they would be settled somewhere safe and supportive as she was completely removed from their life. The social worker was disappointed that I hadn't yet had a change of heart to adopt them myself, I could tell that by her silence on the phone, but she said she'd do what she could. The truth is, each passing day left me more attached to them, and it was all I could do to keep my head on straight: *I want to remain "Aunt Jenny" to the boys, not become "Mom." And I want my turn!*

Dad's criminal and divorce matters weren't moving very quickly either, and I'd yet to decide what I was going to do with the demented man once they were resolved. Should I provide his care myself, free of charge, in my home—forevermore—or should I make him pay out of pocket for 24/7 care in an assisted-living apartment until he's broke? Neither choice felt right. Amid my confusion, as guilt battled resentment about what to do with him, I was assigned to—of all things—a horrific patricide trial. I swore my conscience was mocking me: *My dear, dear Jenny...so you think you're angry with your father? Ha, ha...*

During the proceeding, in color photos projected for the jury on a large screen, I witnessed what a Winchester Magnum .300 traveling at Mach 2.5 can do to the human skull. In this instance, it had formed a temporary cavity in the father's head, then exploded it. Bone fragments shattered the telephone receiver the man had been holding to his ear. The bullet traveled faster than sound, so the party on the other end of the line never heard the blast.

On a short recess in the trial, I called the social worker to see if any progress had been made in finding a home for Kasey and Nick.

The social worker told me that Billy Jack—my stepdad of all people!—and his wife had applied for placement and their home had been approved.

"What? That's not going to work. Billy Jack's not a good possibility." Clarifying the word "wife," I asked, "Is he really married?"

"Yes, they're married."

I'd had no idea. "I know nothing of her, and I have no contact with Billy Jack."

She further explained, "Technically, he's family; kids go to family first."

The hair on the back of my neck stood up. "Did you check his background?"

"Yes."

"Did you see where he just got arrested for transporting marijuana?"

"No, I didn't see that."

"It was in Utah."

"Okay. I'll check."

Once she found that arrest, I was confident Billy Jack getting placement of the boys would be a moot issue. No sooner than I hung up the phone, my work break was over, and I was once again engulfed in that horrific murder trial.

The following Monday, by far the hardest day each week for me, I called the social worker again for an update on prospective placements for the boys. She said Billy Jack was still the only choice.

Confounded by her response, I argued, "But what about the transportation of marijuana?"

"He denied it."

"He denied it? Did you bother to even check for any recent arrests?"

"I couldn't find any."

"He smokes marijuana all the time; what about that?"

"He passed a drug test." There was a pause between us, then she apologized, "I'm sorry, there's nothing I can do."

Feeling coerced by her—*If you don't keep the boys, this is where they'll go*—I vented, "If you'd like to meet in person, I'll tell you exactly what environment they'll be raised in if they go with him." My voice cracked as I got off the phone.

I spent the rest of the day trying to identify one family member who'd be willing to take placement of Kasey and Nick. There was no one. Everybody was either dead or on drugs. The few who walked the straight and narrow had already made it clear they weren't prepared for that type of commitment. Unable to sleep that night, as silly as it sounds, I recalled the California law on self-defense and defense of another: "A defendant is not required to retreat. He or she is entitled to stand his or her ground and defend himself and, if reasonably necessary, to pursue an assailant until the danger has passed. This is so even if safety could have been achieved by retreating." As if a light had switched on, despite the shame I carried from the life I'd been dealt and the less-than-savory choices I'd made, Lady Justice wears a blindfold—I had a right to fight for myself and my great-nephews. We were just as important as the next person—no more, no less.

I called the social worker back the next day and held my ground: "If Billy Jack gets placement, Kasey and Nick will lose all contact with me because I don't associate with him. The boys and I have been together too long; severing our connection will devastate them—and me!"

Still, "I'm sorry, there's nothing I can do."

My hands were tied. An emotional mess, I waited for my great-nephews to be placed with, of all people, my stepdad. To my relief, one week later the social worker phoned me. She said that Sam didn't approve of the placement with Billy Jack either, and that she also would have no contact with him, so she, the social worker, could deny it due to lack of family contact. I thanked the heavens above.

With neither Sam nor Kevin trying to get the boys back, I had to explain to Kasey and Nick that they would be going to a new home—one that was happy and full of love. One that would do fun things and teach them. One that had a mother and a father. One that would allow me to continue to be a great-aunt to them. Coming out of my mouth, that all sounded like a dream come true, but the reality was that, through adoption, I could have lost them forever. I hoped they would get settled into a family that would accept me, too, but I knew their new parents would have the final say. As I prepared for the day Kasey and Nick would transition into a new home, I felt a sickness coming on...self-diagnosed as "Loss." Marked by symptoms of euphoric childhood memories of loved ones seeping to the top of my heart followed by grief of their passing, "Loss" was no friend of mine.

Unaware what the future had in store for the three of us, when opportunities presented themselves, I planted seeds within my great-nephews. After all, who better to teach them how dangerous drugs are than I? At bedtime one evening, I asked both boys, "You know who Superman is, right?"

They answered, "Yes."

"He flies so fast around the world and saves it and his girl Lois

Lane. He's faster than a speeding bullet, more powerful than a locomotive, and able to leap tall buildings in a single bound!"

"Yes!"

I had their attention. "Anyone know his weakness?"

They thought about it for a while, then each finally answered, "No."

"Anyone know what he's afraid of?"

Nick burst out, "Zombies!"

Really? Still? "Nope. Superman's not afraid of zombies, but zombies are afraid of him. Superman's only weakness is radioactive rock called kryptonite. He's strong enough to throw huge boulders to the moon, but if kryptonite is anywhere near him, he gets weak and sick. Until he finds the strength to escape from its hold, it steals all his power and completely takes over his brain. And sadly, it makes him forget all the people he loves—even Lois Lane! There's nothing he can do about it either, except to stay far, far away from kryptonite, because it is just way too powerful—even for Superman.

"Kasey, Nick, that's what drugs do: they make people sick by taking over their heart and brain. People who use drugs forget who they love...and are completely powerless over it." The boys, sitting quietly, were all ears.

Then I asked, "Wanna know a secret? The only thing in this entire world that I'm afraid of is drugs."

Suddenly, Nick jumped off the bottom bunk to the floor: "Aunt Jenny, Aunt Jenny, I will do my special moves and chop those drugs' heads off!"

Loving his animated gestures, I laughed. "Oh, good, good,

Nick! That makes me happy! That makes me *so* happy!"

Kasey's and Nick's beautiful hearts intensified my "Loss" symptoms, daily. While singing our favorite bedtime song—The Dixie Chicks' "Godspeed"—together one evening, "Dragon tails and the water is wide, pirates sail and lost boys fly," Nick interrupted: "Aunt Jenny, do you know what's my favorite part of that song?"

"What?" I asked.

"God hears amen wherever we are."

Kasey agreed.

I did my best to hold back tears. "Yep, that's my favorite part, too."

On a different night, before drifting off to sleep, Kasey remained silent while Nick delivered a crushing, "Aunt Jenny, I want to live with you *and* my mom and dad."

———

November 7, 2013—D-Day—the court hearing on termination of parental rights and freeing up Kasey and Nick for adoption had finally arrived. Sam hadn't visited them in over two months; Kevin in over thirteen—not since the boys were in the emergency shelter. I assumed the hearing would go quickly and awaited the social worker's call to let me know our next steps. However, what she reported to me was that, much to everyone's surprise, Kevin showed up, and the judge granted the matter a continuance of three weeks. At the next court date, both Kevin and Sam appeared; they were contesting the termination of their rights. The matter was continued for a month and a half. After that, it was continued for one week. In one week, it was continued for two weeks due to an emergency. I was told it could take up to a year for a final decision. The older the boys got, the less adoptable they would become, as most people prefer babies. Still, I wanted the boys with me until they had a permanent home, whenever and wherever that may be; I was sticking with them until the end.

Whether it was the stars above, God himself, or simply my mind playing tricks on me, weird things started happening. Once, between court dates, I was driving to town when I passed Kevin on the side of the road. Unusually attired in white linen flowing-in-the-wind pants, he was hitchhiking in the opposite direction from where I was going. A bit farther down the road was a group of four homeless people doing the same.

Several weeks later, I passed a stick of a girl on a bicycle. Dressed in layers of cast-off-looking clothing, she had blond hair that was long and shiny. As if she was incognito, she hid behind large sunglasses, but I was sure it was Sam. Later that night I learned that she had been in the hospital in police custody but had absconded—hence the large sunglasses.

Then, after not having heard from or seen Jonny since I walked past him right after my mom died, a few days after running into an old mutual friend of ours at the bank, I passed him in a car on the road. Not even a week later, a family member friend shared a picture of him on Facebook, and when someone asked her where she'd gotten the dated photo, she posted, "I think I got it from Jenny," meaning me! She hadn't.

The Jonny coincidences didn't end with Facebook. In a rental car, I tried to link my cell phone to its Bluetooth, and the single name to pop up on the car's screen read, of course, "Jonny's" cell. I'm sure it wasn't the same person, but still. And one day while I waited for Kasey and Nick to come out of their school, a man parked behind me on a motorcycle. Wearing Levi's and a T-shirt, straddling his bike, each hand gripping the handlebars, his arms looked remarkably the same as Jonny's used to. I couldn't see his face—he wore dark sunglasses and a black helmet—but his stance was dead on. The same thing happened when I was waiting in a drive-thru at a pharmacy, except I was parked behind a car driven by a man in a backward baseball cap. Fair-skinned and strong, the arm that reached for the meds at the window looked exactly like the one that had once held me. When the man turned to leave, however, it wasn't Jonny. Shaking my head, all I could wonder was, *Am I okay?*

I hadn't lost my mind, thank God; what happened on February 20, 2014, proved it. However, having recently written in my memoir about my childhood at Grandma Maggie's house, more specifically, watching *Sesame Street* on her living room floor and singing along to "One of These Kids Is Doing His Own Thing," the day about threw me for a loop.

On February 20, 2014, Jonny was calendared in one courtroom to be sentenced on a misdemeanor domestic violence charge.

Sam and Kevin were calendared in a second courtroom for their parental rights to Kasey and Nick. (They never showed up—of course.)

Matt's and my son was calendared in a third courtroom to be arraigned on drug charges.

I was in a fourth courtroom reporting a matricide jury trial. There was my conscience again: *My dear, dear Jenny...aren't you angry at your mom, too? Ha, ha...* The victim mother had "no less than 43 stab wounds," mostly to her face. To add to the creepiness of the day, the investigating officer on the case was the same one who responded and authored the coroner's report at my own mother's death; the forensic pathologist was the same one who had performed her autopsy.

I wanted to run to the safety of my bed the minute I got home that evening and wake up the next day to find the past sixteen months had been just a bad dream. Resting, however, wasn't an option for me: I had Dad, Kasey, and Nick to look after.

———

Dad had always been about himself—he even had his own name tattooed on his upper arm. "I-V-A-N. I paid four bucks for it when I was in the military," he often bragged. At sixty-nine, he hadn't changed a bit either; he was all take and no give.

My father spent his waking hours ruminating over his marital separation, which caused him great distress. Nearly every day I'd come home from work to: "I think I'm just going to file for divorce."

And nearly every day I would respond, "Dad, she's already filed."

"We're getting a divorce then?"

"Yes."

Then he would get angry. "Oh. Well, why does she get everything? Half that house is mine. She can't just have everything."

"I know, Dad. That's why you have an attorney."

"She was the one fucking the neighbor."

"Right, Dad."

Then he'd quote, almost to the dollar, the amount in his 401k. He never forgot *that*.

Other days, even though I unfailingly gave him his monthly bank statements, I'd come home to find he'd rummaged through all his papers trying to figure out if I'd misused any of his money. I'd print him a copy of his current account activity, he'd scrutinize it closely, then act like he wasn't accusing me of wrongdoing.

As a piece of their divorce settlement, Dad and Pat had agreed to swap vehicles. She got the sedan back and he got the pickup. Dad's health made him a hazard on the road, so his truck sat for months in my driveway. I loaned my car to Tony, my son, so I asked to borrow Dad's rig until I got mine back. Reluctantly, he said, "Okay." Two weeks later, I was driving him to The Waffle Shop for his weekly outing when I noticed he was disgruntled. We'd barely hit the road before he leaned over and asked, "How many miles are on this now?"

I looked down, then looked over at him and said, "22,898."

He shook his head and sighed like I was racking up the mileage on it.

Sarcastically, I added, "Not bad for a truck that's nine years old." He said no more, just stared out the passenger window the entire way there and back. Most days, Dad's self-centeredness wore through my patience. I didn't want to be a mean person— after all, he did suffer from dementia—but the truth was I was still angry at him for his past with my mom. Sometimes I wondered if *this* was the lowest point in his life rather than when he was with her, like he had told me. I knew that someday I would be faced with a decision: Do I take care of him or take care of me?

I checked into assisted-living apartments for I-V-A-N. Those started at a whopping $3,100 a month, but someone would be available 24/7 to fulfill his needs. The complex's manager urged me to put Dad on their secured facility's waiting list for when he started to wander. She explained, "We rarely have openings there due to the number of baby boomers with dementia." *Those damn baby boomers.*

Writing was still my only escape, and I continued to push through the process. When I'd gone as far as I could on paper, I purchased word processing software and learned how to use it. *Smoke Rings Rising* became a convenient computer file—with cut and paste. I felt like a journalist following an important story, except that story was my own, and I had no idea how it would end.

Unexpectedly, I got a call from my brother Brian, who lived in Washington. He said he'd be passing through our area later that day and wanted to drop in for a visit. I hadn't seen him since Mom's funeral; I was stoked. When he arrived, I introduced him to my dad. That was odd, when I thought about it.

Our evening was spent catching up and telling stories from our childhoods. Since my brother and I shared next to none of our youth together, all but one of our stories involving Mom, Teresa, and Lori were from our separate upbringings. Brian said, "Yeah, I couldn't believe it; I came to visit Mom once and there were little kids walking around with joints!"

"That was probably me."

"Was it?"

"*Highly* likely." I laughed.

Brian, given Washington's recent legalization of recreational marijuana, said he was working hard at opening his own dispensary. He assured me, "There are strict guidelines regarding kids and marijuana in the recreational realm." For that I was grateful.

We spoke of Teresa. I gave him the rundown that she had spent eighteen months in prison in San Joaquin County for petty crimes, failures to appear, and failures to pay that eventually caught up with her, but she did come out of it with a GED. I told him she had been living in a homeless community under a bridge for more than five years; and each year, as the weather turned cold, I'd get a dreadful knot in my stomach. I explained how once I finagled a travel trailer to get her out of the elements and had planned to pack it with food and toiletries for her. All she had to do was find a place to put it. She couldn't. With a hopeless look on his face, I sensed Brian, like me, was at a loss about how to help her.

Brian's visit was just that, passing through, but it was special. Given his above-average height, blond hair, and blue eyes, he undeniably was a full blood-related sibling to Teresa and Lori. Given my short height, brown hair—now with a touch of gray!— and brown eyes, I undeniably was not. Still, none of the biological stuff mattered; by the end of the evening, he was my big brother and I was his "Sis."

It had been at least a year since I had heard from Teresa, but shortly after Brian's visit, she called me from Stockton. She was happy to share she'd recently moved into a trailer in a mobile home park with a friend. That was great news; knowing she'd be out of winter's elements, maybe that annual knot in my stomach would subside. Asking about Billy Jack, she wailed, "He promised Momma he'd take care of me after she was gone. He used to bring me food, but I haven't seen him since he re-married." Per Sam, who when she was drug-free had delivered meals to Teresa, you had to follow a trail off the road and step under a barbed wire fence among transients to get to her home-less camp. That was far too scary of an adventure for this girl, even to help my sister. Billy Jack had, in fact, taken care of Te-resa from time to time, but I didn't have an explanation for her as to why he had stopped.

During our conversation, Teresa and I discussed Sam's boys. She asked: "How come you're not going to keep them?" Before I could answer, in a matter-of-fact tone, she added, "You just take care of your own, huh?"

Whatever. I offered her no response.

My sister's call was perfectly timed, however, because I had so many questions that only she could answer. I started with, "Teresa, who was Mom with when I was born?"

"She was with nobody, Sissy. Nobody was there for her. She was with Ivan, but he was with every other woman in town."

Seemed fitting. "Who told her to call a cab when she went into labor with me?"

"Ivan. She had stayed over with him. When she went into labor, he asked her if she had her own money to call a cab."

Seemed fitting as well, but now I was irritated. I continued my questioning: "Okay. Who used to cut her nightgown off her?"

Almost boasting, "That was Willy. He'd use his switchblade

and cut it off without leaving a scratch on her."

I was not amused. "Okay. And who wanted to buy me at five years old?"

As if she was recalling a happy memory, "Oh, yeah, somebody wanted to buy you for a hundred thousand dollars or something; I can't remember the exact amount."

"Ten thousand dollars," I said. "Now I remember. Mom said somebody wanted to buy me for ten thousand. But, Teresa, 'buy' can mean a lot of things."

"It was a family. A family wanted to buy you, Sissy."

I thanked God. All those years I'd thought some kind of pedophile—or pervert—had wanted to buy me. I took two large breaths, then continued, "Do you know who molested Lori at eight years old?"

"Lori was molested at eight years old?"

"Yes. She told me that she was molested at eight but didn't say who did it."

"I don't know anything about that."

"Well, Mom married Willy in 1973, when Lori would have been eight. I found out online that he was arrested for molesting a three-year-old. Could he have done it?"

Teresa paused as she tried to think back. Then, certain of her answer, replied, "No, no, he wasn't like that. I never got that feeling from him. Was he convicted?"

"I don't know."

"No, it wasn't him. He wasn't like that." She continued, "You were Willy's buddy, though. He loved you. You'd stand up next to him in the front seat of the car in your overalls, and you guys would pass a bottle of vodka or Jack, I can't remember which one now, back and forth."

Given that I was two-ish when Mom and he married, Lord, did eerie thoughts race through my mind.

I made sure to leave my conversation with Teresa on a happy, positive note just in case I never heard from her again. She said she'd call me on the following weekend...she didn't.

———

When I was sure that Kasey and Nick were going to need a family again, because Kevin and Sam still wouldn't cooperate with Child Protective Services, I retraced my steps. Afraid that I might open an old wound, I hesitantly called my first choice in Colorado—Marie. To my surprise, it turned out that she had spent the past nine months filling out papers, having background checks, taking all the necessary classes, and doing whatever she needed to do to become a certified fost-adopt home. She was elated to receive my message. It turned out that my first choice was the right choice. I contacted the social worker to let her know that Marie had had a change of heart. And when it was a possibility that she would be considered for placement, I loosely questioned Kasey and Nick on how they felt about her. Neither gave me a response.

Another time, driving my great-nephews home from school—seventeen months since their initial detention—Nick asked, "Aunt Jenny, when is my mom going to pick us up? It's been a long, long time."

All I could say was, "I know, honey." Car rides had been a

great setting for our conversations in the past, and although I had broached the issue with them before, my choice to bring it up then and there wasn't the best. I asked, "Remember how we talked about you boys possibly moving in with Marie in Colorado? Well, I learned from the social worker today that that might be what is going to happen." I paused, then asked, "How do you feel about that?"

Nick got enraged with his seatbelt for locking on him, again, then started to cry. Kasey asked about the school he'd go to in Colorado, whether it was better than his current one. I tried to verbally console Nick and told Kasey the school in Colorado was an excellent one, like his was, but in a much better place. I gently explained that their parents had been gone a long time, and that kids can't wait until they're eighteen before their parents get it together; they need to have a family—and a childhood. The boys fell silent.

In the days that followed, my great-nephews started asking me questions about Colorado and Marie, so I knew they were processing the idea of moving. Once things started happening with their placement, I was sure it would occur quickly, so to help them develop a relationship with Marie before they moved, rather than after, I scheduled a trip to visit her—and this time they knew why.

Marie—and Colorado—was a hit with my great-nephews, but now that they were aware they'd be moving from my home, the boys' nightmares and the many insecurities we had worked through resurfaced. Kasey felt victimized again at school; and Nick started gathering up his weapons before he went to sleep at night—his sword, but especially his gun. Hoping to fix what I started, I explained, "Nick, Uncle Matt doesn't have a gun because he is afraid—he is not afraid—he only has a gun for hunting." I don't know that he understood.

Marie took the initiative to call the boys every day, which was my saving grace because she had a calming effect over them—even while they slept. *Whew!* Sometimes they would talk for hours. Kasey often walked around the house with her on speakerphone—inside, outside, in the shower, on the toilet—it didn't matter where. Nick was standoffish at first, but soon warmed up to her, too. That was clear the day I saw him outside on the phone, staring at the ground and walking in circles, singing for her, "We Are Young," his favorite song at that time.

Notwithstanding the distance between them, by way of the daily telephone calls and sometimes Skype, Marie successfully created a genuine connection with Kasey and Nick. It was sweet to watch them light up—and even argue about who would talk first—every time she called. At bedtime one night, Kasey divulged, "Aunt Jenny, if Marie picks us up, I'll be all right; but I am still going to miss my mom and dad."

Nick asked, "Is Marie going to be our mom?"

"Yes, your 'forever' mom," I answered, "someone who'll always be there for you no matter what."

Kasey asserted, "I'm all right with that."

Nick agreed. "Me, too. Aunt Jenny, I love you *and* Marie."

On a second trip to Colorado, we stayed at Marie's home. Given the reason we were there was to familiarize my great-nephews with what I hoped would become their new home and community, I was happy yet overwhelmed on the first day of our stay, so I called it an early night. The boys stayed up and visited with Marie. Right before a sleepy Nick went to what would become his new bottom bunk in his new shared bedroom with his brother—she'd had it all set up and ready for them—he opened the door to my room and came in to give me a squeeze of a hug. That night, I had the most vivid dream that he had crawled into bed with me. I awoke reaching for him. It made for a rough day on my part, but I knew my decision for Kasey and Nick would mean a great future full of many opportunities. After a two-night stay, we headed back to California, as their case was still in process.

Marie and I planned get-togethers, as many as we could afford anyway, to give her more time with the boys—we did live almost twelve hundred miles apart. After our Colorado excursion, Marie committed to flying to California for the four of us to visit Disneyland. The boys had grown a bit taller since our last trip there, which meant they could enjoy more rides. To say they were looking forward to it is an understatement.

"Two days until Disneyland, boys! Yay!" (I couldn't wait either.)

Kasey, excited about our vacation, asked, "Aunt Jenny, did you buy those songs yet?"

Playing with him, I answered, "Oh, I don't know. Which ones were they again? How do they go?"

"One goes, 'Ready, set, go; ready, set, go.' The other is, 'It's the final countdown.'"

"Yes, I bought them for you. By the way, did you know that 'Ready, Set, Go' is a Christian song?"

"Yes."

"Really? Where did you hear it? I've never heard it before."

"On the radio."

"Oh, I'll bet on Uncle Matt's radio. And 'The Final Count-down' is almost thirty years old! That's by a group called Europe. Where did you hear that one?"

"At the afterschool program."

"It sounds sort of like the song in *Rocky*. Do you know who Rocky is?"

Kasey shook his head.

"He was a boxer in a movie. They made, I think, five *Rocky* films? I watched the very first one in the theater with your grand-ma when we were kids. They are good. Maybe we should watch them all while you're here." We never did get around to it.

Marie flew into town, and two days later the boys, their Aunt Stephanie and Uncle Steven and their families, Marie, and I all caravanned down to Disneyland and spent four days together. Ka-sey and Nick chose Marie over me to take them on all the rides—except Indiana Jones; Kasey and I had made an earlier pact to ride that one together since he was finally tall enough. I happily tagged along—witnessing the beautiful bond between a mother and her children develop—and shot pictures of the three. Being sneaky, my great-nephews posed atop Disneyland's Tomorrowland sculp-ture for me...a photo that will forever melt my heart.

On our last night in the park, I watched the fireworks show alone on a bench as I waited for Kasey, Nick, and Marie to return from one of the souvenir shops. Marie had promised the boys "ears," aka Mickey Mouse hats, before we left. There was that shooting star again, the one from the year before that sparked Nick's request: "I wish my mom and dad would pick us up." Although still painful to think about, I was in a peaceful place; the boys were, too.

The next morning, Marie caught a flight back to Colorado; the rest of us headed home to northern California.

With adoption for my great-nephews underway and the decision made to move my dad into his own assisted-living apartment—yep—Matt and I were assessing what our home's next remodel project should be and determined that its dry-rotted, second-story deck was now a hazard. Our plan to replace it, as well as the siding and the rest of the windows, had been at a standstill since the day I received Kasey and Nick from the emergency shelter, and further delayed because Dad showed up at our door. We decided to hire my step-brother Lonny to help us with the project.

The plant-by-number drought-tolerant flower gardens we had planted had been a wise move, because they continued to grow and bloom despite the past year and a half or better of neglect. Surprisingly, the recently planted fastidious Matilija poppy was still with us—in its heart-shaped hole Matt had dug—and budding! I waited weeks for the first bloom, checking its progress daily. Then it happened: delicate, snow-white petals surrounding a bright yellow-orange center. It was stunning. I walked proudly into the house to tell Kasey and Nick, who had been waiting for the bloom, too. Suddenly I realized what day it was. Shaking my head, I mentioned to Kasey, "The Matilija bloomed...on your mom's [Sam's] birthday."

We double-checked the calendar, which read May twenty-seventh, and looked at each other like, *Whoa*.

June 2014, Kasey and Nick were on the court's calendar for my request that they go out of state to stay with Marie while Matt and I went on our upcoming anniversary road trip. Finding the boys a sitter for longer than a day was still next to impossible. In addition to granting my request, the judge allowed them an extended, if not permanent, visit with her and set the termination of parental rights hearing for November.

Marie flew to California to gather her boys and partake in their "blast-off" party; a lovely afternoon shared with family and friends. The three left the following morning for Colorado—both boys wearing their Halloween skeleton suits and masks. Kasey was, for the most part, all smiles; Nick, on the other hand, wouldn't acknowledge me—no goodbye kiss or farewell pictures. It was like I was dead to him, and it killed me.

By evening, I had Dad moved into his new assisted-living apartment. I knew if I didn't do it that day, I wouldn't have been able to do it at all.

CHAPTER FIFTEEN

AFTERBURN

How could she not know...what she was doing?

I awoke with a heavy heart because of Nick's refusal to hug, kiss, or even let me snap a picture of him before he left with Marie. Still, I was happy for him and Kasey; I knew they were going to be forever loved, live in a great place, and had an amazing future ahead of them. Matt had left at sunup for a bass tournament in Clearlake. My plan for the day was to attend a family gathering that included Millie, and then go to Zack's birthday celebration; my firstborn was now a whopping twenty-six. That evening, I'd unwind with my husband, in our now empty nest, then start the ten-day countdown to a much-needed reprieve: national park hopping for our twelve-year anniversary.

I stepped out of bed feeling like I'd been beat up—or run over by a train and dragged across the country—and extremely tired. The morning seemed to move in slow motion, and so did I, but I made it to the afternoon family get-together. Surprisingly, Millie behaved. She didn't really have an opportunity to act out, however, because I had to leave early to make it to Zack's house. Still tired, once his party was over, I made my way back home. I arrived at Matt's "My mom called looking for you."

"Why? What now?"

"I don't know. She didn't want to talk to *me*; she wanted to talk to *you*."

"That's funny; she didn't bother calling my cell phone. What, was she tattling to you that I left the gathering early?"

"I don't know."

"I went to Zack's, for his party, which is what I told you I was going to do."

Millie was just keeping tabs on me because she thought Matt was out of town, which was her M.O. Every year, Matt spent opening weekend of deer season hunting with his father and, like clockwork, I'd receive nightly calls from her...to make sure I was honoring her son in his absence, I suppose. Why else?

I walked my frustration with Millie off, because I was just too tired to deal with her at that time. I waited until later.

While cooking dinner, I thought it would be a good idea to clear the air about Matt's mother so we could start that evening, as well as the days ahead, free of pent-up resentments. Gently, I brought up Millie calling the house for me. Matt still didn't have an answer as to why she did so. I told him about a comment she'd recently posted on my public Facebook profile picture that I felt was possessive and inappropriate: "If anyone out there doesn't know, Jenn's my daughter-in-law, married to my son, and is such an amazing woman." I opened my Facebook page and showed him the anything-but-provocative photo. He scrutinized it, then responded, "It really doesn't look like you're a married woman."

My jaw dropped with surprise in that it sounded like he was siding with his mother. "I can be married *and* be my own person." He said nothing more. Just before closing out my page, I noticed a friend request from our accountant. I had no intention of accepting it and told Matt that; he appeared unmoved. As far as I could tell, all was right with the world; we sat down at the dining room table and enjoyed a cozy meal together.

After dinner, on a perfect June night—not too hot—Matt and I hung out on our deck-in-progress that he and Lonny had been working on. I lay my head down on the marbled, rich brown composite wood planks and, at peace, stared at the stars. *Thy turn hath arrived!*

No sooner had that thought crossed my mind than I picked up edgy vibes from Matt. "What's up?" I asked.

Returning to the topic of the Facebook friend request from our accountant, he said, "It's not you that I don't trust, but everyone else."

Short-fused (apparently), that was all it took to set me off. Deemed weak, vulnerable, untrustworthy, and incompetent—all seeds planted by Millie—a fit of fury befell me such that I could have exorcised Linda Blair myself. I wanted to hurt my mother-in-law for dividing her son and me—again. I drilled into Matt: "I hate your family! Treat me like I'm second class? Fuck them! I'll be damned if I'm sitting in the back of the bus! Fuck you and fuck them!" I made my way through the house to our bedroom, slamming doors and screaming at the top of my lungs, "I'm done!" I didn't break anything, but I wanted to—every single thing we had built together; because if I wasn't respected and trusted, all of it was worthless. Matt stood silent. I went to bed.

The next morning, all I could do was suck it up, as did Matt, and look forward to Friday, the Fourth of July. That was the start of our anniversary trip. We were flying to Idaho to visit Matt's childhood best friend, Pete, and then driving through Glacier, Yellowstone, and Grand Teton National Parks. This breath of fresh air was exactly what Matt and I needed.

Under clear blue skies in Idaho, with Pete and his wife Ruthie, we rode quad runners looking for wildlife tracks, picking wild huckleberries and strawberries along the way for late-afternoon homemade milkshakes. The following day, the four of us visited Montana's Glacier National Park. Convoying along Going-to-the-Sun Road, we passed Lake McDonald, Heavens Peak, the Weeping Wall, and the Jackson Glacier, to name a few natural wonders. From that park, Pete and Ruthie returned home to Idaho; Matt and I continued to Yellowstone. There we meandered through travertine limestone terraces, saw bison and a momma bear with cubs, visited the Petrified Tree, Grand Canyon, Old Faithful, and the Grand Prismatic Spring. Our last adventure was through Grand Teton National Park, where, under the majestic scenery of the youngest mountain range of the Rockies, we were fortunate enough to spot a moose cow and her calf romping through a slow-running stream.

Our road trip ended at Jenny Lake Lodge, where we'd rented a cozy cabin, "Forget Me Not," for our final night's stay. In the lodge's rustic dining area, we were seated at a table for two next to a window with a perfect view of the Tetons. Matt wore a dinner jacket and Wranglers; I had on a cute but classy dress with heels. Under soft lighting from the overhead lamp, my husband looked at me in a way that I can't explain, but he sat back, didn't say a word, and just smiled at me without intrusion. I, too, stayed silent. In the quiet, without my family's turmoil, without his family's subjugation, with all our adult kids safe and sound, it was just us. I realized, *This is it...my turn.*

Revived after our much-needed sight-seeing adventure, I hit the ground running when I got home, right into what I called my "defensible space"—Calgon baths and music—and made my emotional health a priority. Immersed in the fragrant, hot water and my favorite songs, I spent many evenings reflecting upon my childhood family members. The hard truth was how they ended up: Mom, an overdose at fifty-nine; Lori, a meth-related fatal car crash at thirty-three; Teresa, homeless (again) at fifty. I reflected upon Sam's complete U-turn—in the wrong direction—and the past twenty-one months I'd spent with Kasey and Nick. I reflected upon Jonny, "Was it me, or meth?" With Matt, it had always been me and nothing else. I reflected upon Millie, the woman hell-bent on dividing my marriage yet keeping it intact for 'God's' sake. And I reflected upon the day Tim, as if he were Clint Eastwood, just before glancing over at his bottom drawer that may or may not have housed his pistol, directed, "You have to protect yourself." He was right.

Tim now lived out of state, but to a handful of his long-timers—like me—he remained available via Skype. I had questions I needed answered and, given our long history together, he was the only one who could help me. The day I called to set up a session, I warned, "Shrapnel—blood spatter everywhere!" We briefly spoke about what my great-nephews and I had been through and how the painful situation had dovetailed into a memoir manuscript. He was pleased to hear I was writing and offered to read my work. I emailed it to him before our first Skype session.

When Tim and I resumed counseling, he appeared on the computer screen in a M*A*S*H shirt. I appreciated the levity. His "Imagine" placard in the background and Bill, his metal statue, standing tall in front of his display of degrees along the wall were comforting—like old times. I jumped right in, "Tim, years ago you told me my mother had no idea what she was doing. How could she not know what she was doing?" He asked for further details, beyond what he'd read in my manuscript, of Mom's family of origin. I told him all I knew and let him in on her "what happened to me" disclosure: as an adolescent, she was molested by her sister's husband.

He shook his head for a few moments, then explained, "You know, Jenny, life is really all about connections."

"Okay. So Mom obviously didn't have a good one with her hard-ass—*sorry*—father."

"Yes; the most important person to a little girl. Without a connection with him, it was difficult for her to develop the trust and acceptance that would give her the self-esteem to navigate life in a healthy way."

"Grandma overcompensated for Grandpa's harshness, didn't she? Like when Mom would sneak out of the house and Grandma would cover for her?"

"Your mom learned at a very young age how to maneuver her way through their system. Without accountability within a balanced pair of parents, instead of gaining self-confidence and autonomy to grow into a successful and industrious woman, your mom developed doubt and dependence and unhealthy survival skills."

"Mom was smart, wanted to become an architect or writer. Instead, she spent her entire adult life on some form of aid. After welfare, when all of us kids were grown, she applied and was granted SSI, Social Security Income, for, in part, 'lack of employability.' Her life was wasted."

"During her adolescence, when she was supposed to develop a strong, positive identity, she instead developed helplessness, confusion, and shame—"

"When 'what happened to her' happened to her."

"When she was violated by your uncle, yes."

"Mom said Aunt Jeannie blamed her; said it was her fault. She probably carried guilt, huh, for *his* unconscionable actions?"

"More than likely, yes."

"Add to that bipolar disorder amid the influences of the sixties and seventies."

"As a young adult, she sought that missing connection with her father through men—"

"Married and pregnant at age sixteen."

"—and later drugs, identifying herself sexually and/or being 'just a drug addict.' Continuing in that vein without intervention, instead of seeking interaction with peers, she isolated herself. And being an isolated, emotionally and developmentally delayed young mother who was lacking a strong connection with someone, she connected with her own children in a harmful way."

"Engaging in substance use with them."

"Yes."

"A half a century later, subsequent generations of my family still suffer."

"Exactly."

There was a long pause between us before I concluded, "Underneath all the layers of mental illness and addiction, Tim, my mom's heart was good, though."

Making sure he had my full attention by cramming his face into his computer's camera, "I'm sure of it."

"Because she gave me mine."

"She did."

"And had she been successfully treated, she probably would have been a remarkable writer."

"You bet."

I laughed. "Of course, she would have...she was her daughter's mother."

———

The road to healing wasn't an easy one and—yet again—my conscience was there to guide me through it. This time I was assigned to a child sexual molestation trial. The brown-haired, brown-eyed alleged victim, now a senior in high school, testified in front of the jury for hours regarding the allegations against her stepdad; the only physical evidence she had was her handwritten disclosure of the charged offense which she'd given to her counselor.

Midtrial, when experts in child sexual abuse testified, my jaw about hit the floor. "It's easier for kids to disclose abuse in writing rather than in person...it's easier for kids to disclose abuse after they are removed from the abusive situation...seeing others being victimized sometimes triggers a disclosure." I wondered what Tim thought when he read the first draft of my memoir; after all our time together, up until then, he'd known only half my story.

On the last day of evidence, the alleged victim was called up again to testify. When there were no further questions from either side, the youthful girl stepped down from the witness stand. As she left the well of the courtroom and passed in front of the jurors, then the attorneys, and finally through the audience, each step got longer and more pronounced, and her head raised a little higher. When she pushed through those huge mahogany doors, I couldn't help but notice the rows of family and friends, some with pursed lips, sitting in support of the defendant. On the other side only one person was seated: the state's Victim-Witness advocate. After deliberations, the jury returned a guilty verdict.

Then, I was assigned to the child dependency courtroom wherein two brothers—Kasey and Nick look-alikes—were the stars of the show on their adoption day. Go figure. With the room full of family and friends, the lively boys emceed for us everything we ever wanted to know about dinosaurs in every crazy voice imaginable. They gave quite the performance. I left the courthouse feeling reassured that I'd made the right decision regarding my great-nephews and was thankful I'd be seeing them soon.

My conscience continued to astound me. In September, keeping my promise to Nick, I was packing for a flight to Colorado to attend a party for his sixth birthday. I remembered both boys had forgotten their Mickey Mouse hats from our last Disneyland trip. The hats were more than just souvenirs, they were a promise kept by their soon-to-be "forever" mom. With no room in my suitcase, the only choice I had was to drape them over the handle.

At the Sacramento International Airport, with one large Mickey Sorcerer Hat and one small Mickey Ears Hat dangling from my bag, I was the second-to-last person to board the Southwest flight. I shuffled through feet and elbows within the aisle to my seat, which was the left side middle of the last row. I put my case in the storage bin above and sat down with the ears resting on top of my travel purse.

Within minutes of getting settled into my spot, I heard a faint gasp from the young man in the seat to the right of me, which, from my perspective, was the very last seat in the entire plane. I heard the gasp again. He was distraught over something. I looked around to see if anybody else had heard him. The flight attendant walked past, and I wondered if I should alert her. As the engines revved to prepare for take-off, he spread open his right hand and placed it over the glass of the window.

Finally, I asked him, "Are you okay?"

He glanced at me, surprised that anyone had noticed that he was upset, and said, "Yeah."

I could tell he was of Asian descent, but unable to discern

whether he was a teenager or adult. A few minutes later, the engines revved up again and we started to take off. He continued to stare out the window, and then I heard his gasp turn into full-on crying, but he was trying hard to hide it. His hand on the window he moved back and forth—clenched to flat.

I asked if I could get him something to drink.

He said, "No, thank you. I already have something."

Trying to strike up a conversation and hopefully ameliorate the situation, I asked if he was afraid of flying. He looked over at me and openly explained, "No, I'm not afraid of flying. I'm leaving my mom for the first time to go live with my father in another state. My parents are divorced."

"Oh, geez. I'm so sorry. That's tough." I paused for a moment, then inquired, "Can I ask how old you are?"

"I'm only fourteen." He continued, "I'm very close to my mother, but not so much my father. I'm really going to miss her." He said he hated that he now had to fly a total of thirteen times a year and just wished his parents lived close enough, like in the same town, to be able to drive to see each other.

By then I had a huge knot in my throat and was trying to hold back my own tears. I told him how sincerely sorry I was for his situation and explained that my mom had been married five times—he interrupted, "Really? Five times?"—and not to my real father either.

"Wow, my problems aren't so bad then."

"No, no, they are." I added, "I'm not trying to make light of your situation; it is very sad." I told him about the past two years with my great-nephews, Kasey and Nick, how they lost both their parents to drugs and were being adopted. I showed him the Mickey Mouse ears and explained that I was going to see them.

He gave me a soft smile, took it all in, and then said, "I'm going to stop crying."

"No, no, cry. I've been crying for two years. Get it all out so you can heal."

"Really?"

I said, "Yes," and I meant it.

Our conversation seemed to calm the boy down.

Once the plane landed, I turned to him, "Can I say just one more thing?"

In a much better mood, he answered, "Yeah."

"You seem to be such a good kid. Things in life are going to happen that are very hard, just don't let them make you angry. Try your best to stay focused and on track with your goals. Know that it will get better."

He smiled again and said, "Okay."

I gathered my suitcase from the bin above—he stayed seated because he had to go on to another state—and I placed, once again, the Mickey Mouse hats over my suitcase handle, after showing them to him one last time. He smiled and said, "Thank you."

Marie picked me up at the Denver International Airport, and as we drove to gather Kasey and Nick from their school, I couldn't help but think about the boy on the plane—and how much I missed my own mother. Marie could tell I wasn't quite with her, so I explained my flight "details." She understood.

When school let out, I was expecting Nick to race to me,

yelling happily, "Aunt Jenny!" like in the past, but instead, when he approached Marie and me, he acted as if I wasn't there. I was still a nobody to him, I guess. Marie said it was a defense mechanism to avoid his feelings for me. *Ouch*—it still hurt. Kasey, on the other hand, was excited and told everybody in his classroom, "This is my Aunt Jenny!"

Our afternoon together started with a short hiking trip to one of the boys' favorite places, Rock Playground. Along the way, Nick continued to ignore me, but when he cleared a mud puddle, I snapped a photo of him—airborne—anyway. From Rock Playground, we went to their home, where Nick lightened up on me, thankfully. While Marie made dinner, the boys showed me their many toys and shared the projects they were working on. At bedtime, Nick asked to sleep in my bed. Of course, I said yes. By daylight, however, he'd made his way to Marie's, which was a great sign.

Once we were all up and at 'em, Nick's birthday was filled with plans that included a bowling party with lots of friends, pizza, cake, and all sorts of presents—something I wish every kid could have. We retired that evening exhausted and full of junk food. I had a flight to catch back to California the next morning.

As I exited Marie's car at the Southwest Airlines drop-off, I promised to see the boys again in three months—December— for Kasey's birthday. They both replied, "We already know!" Happy boys blew kisses and waved goodbye to me from the inside of their car as I walked through the doors of the airport. I left Denver confident that my great-nephews would continue to thrive with Marie. Permanency for the family finally happened the following year, 2015, on National Adoption Day.

I arrived home to find that Millie was at it again. This time she cast a dark cloud of unfounded rumors about troubles within my marriage. Like she'd delivered a fearful war cry—"Divorce!"—in-laws stopped by unannounced to get, I felt, a sense for how Matt and I were doing. Millie didn't stop by; rather, she'd call and not leave a message when I didn't answer. Twice Matt received word about my whereabouts when I wasn't working during work hours. People associated with his family who didn't care for me—but didn't want Matt to be a two-time divorcee either—started sending me Facebook friend requests. Everyone began "liking" my posts, too, including Millie, who most often ignored them unless she could be condescending. Millie's nonsense triggered Matt's insecurities—the trust ones he'd faced during his first marriage—which, in turn, triggered me. I swore to him, "I'm no longer on this planet to make your family happy, and I will never, ever allow myself to be vulnerable to them again!" That time I shattered a glass bowl on the floor. Matt again stood silent; I again went to bed.

At the next family gathering, Millie had the gall to address me as "The Missus." That evening, I pressed Matt, "Why is your mom treating me like I can't be trusted?"

Obviously still a bit apprehensive about me—*Mother knows best, right?*—he didn't have an answer.

During my next Skype session with Tim, I fumed about my maddening mother-in-law. I cried, "How come I always end up like this? How come I always find myself in controlling situations? How come people always mess with me? I know I've brought on a lot of the difficulties in my life, but how did I do it this time? Why can't I have a smooth, happy life? That's all I've ever wanted!"

"Jennifer, because you *accommodate* people. You learned early in your childhood how to accommodate others. You're a caretaker. You try to make and keep other people happy. You were taught early on to not rock the boat."

Be the bigger person... "And carried it into adulthood."

"Yes. You know, you can go about life without letting difficult people get under your skin...you can only be the victim if you care; right? Remember that?"

"Right. But, Tim, my mother-in-law is Millie."

He laughed. "That goes for her, too. Who cares what she thinks?"

Doubtful I could ever get to that place, I just responded, "All right."

––––––––

Lonny, beating the heat one early Saturday morning, was working on the deck when he mentioned to me, "Jonny said Sam is living down the street from him in someone's garage." *Of course! The once aspiring fireman always shows up during my times of trouble!* Lonny continued, "I paid her a visit and tried to talk her into going home with me, but she refused."

During our last Skype session—that go-round—I asked Tim a long overdue question: "What is it with Jonny and me?"

He thought for a few seconds, then asked, "How long has it been?"

"Almost thirty years since we were together."

He paused a bit longer than I expected. Thinking he might have the wrong idea, I quickly added, "I don't want to sleep with him; it's not like that."

"Oh, I don't think that. What happened, Jenny, is you bonded to him before you had fully emotionally developed. You needed someone so badly to connect with, and you did it with him."

"I trusted him. He said he loved me. I believed him."

"It was special, but it's just a memory."

I laughed through a few tears. "I have a 'biological' boyfriend and a 'forever' husband."

Tim laughed as well, then encouraged me saying, "Jenny, it's never too late to have a happy childhood."

An image of colorful Bobo came to mind. "If only I were a mighty little hummingbird; then I could fly backward and, moving forward, gracefully maneuver around all that now holds me back. I'd return baggage-free."

He smiled. "You can do it."

"Except I'm more like the Matilija poppy: I have trouble getting rooted. Every time I plant my feet, I'm undermined by something—or someone. First came Jonny, then came meth. Next came Matt, then came Millie."

"So, to you, Millie equals meth."

I hadn't thought about it like that, but he made sense. "Yes. And, just like meth, she's lurking around every corner, ready to wreak havoc on my life."

He didn't disagree with me. Instead, he whispered, "A burnt child dreads the fire."

"Huh?"

"I said, 'A burnt child dreads the fire.'"

After processing his perspective, I replied, "Well, perhaps. But you know something about the Matilija?"

"What?"

"It may be difficult for her to get rooted, but once she does, she becomes invasive, delivering the most elegant of blooms you'll ever see. In fact, her beauty often floods fire-stricken lands—as it takes smoke to make her shoot."

Tim brought his fingers to his mouth and chef kissed, "*Mwah!*" Moments later, he reiterated, "Jenny, you *can* do it."

"I hope so."

"It's your turn."

EPILOGUE

Smoke rings, falling...

I thought I was never going to heal, but I did. And I finished my memoir; it almost goes without saying. When I was ready, nearly two years later, I stepped out of my "defensible space" and allowed Dad to move back home. Knowing I'd need an occasional out from taking care of him, Matt and I purchased a used, self-contained pontoon boat. Moored on Lake Oroville, it was a mere ten minutes from our house, and came in especially useful the following July.

Seven-seven-seventeen—I call it "the day of completion." It was a Friday and a record 107 degrees. While I was at work, I received news that the recently ignited Wall Fire was burning uncontrollably through mountainy east Oroville—and only two miles from Matt's and my residence. I left the courthouse early and went home to pack important papers, pictures, clothes, and Dad's plethora of medications into my car, just in case the firefighters couldn't contain the blaze and it reached us. Matt left his job early, too, and spent the afternoon reinforcing firebreaks with his backhoe and cutting brush to touch up his "defensible space" around our home. He kept watch as the wildfire lingered just over the next ridge from us.

Seven-eight-seventeen—"the day of new beginnings." Burning just over twenty-four hours, the still uncontained fire had consumed 2,700 acres. Matt continued to track it, as it now had crested the ridge. With air tankers and helicopters carrying water buckets dousing the flames nonstop, I was sure the firefighters would gain control over it before it reached us, but if not, my plan was to drop Dad and his dog Misty off at the assisted-living facility he'd previously stayed at, and Matt, our dog Dottie, and I would take refuge in our pontoon boat on the lake.

While serving Dad dinner, I looked out his window and noticed a change in the smoke; it had turned dark and was extremely close. My father walked, barely, with a walker, so transporting him anywhere was always a struggle—and slow. Realizing it would be next to impossible to get him out in a hurry, I thought it best we get a head start. I'm glad I did, because—moving at a snail's pace—I'd no sooner gotten him seated in my car and his legs swung around to the floorboard when I heard a loud horn blow, then fire personnel announce: "An immediate evacuation is necessary." I quickly belted Dad and put Misty on his lap; Dottie jumped in the rear. Matt, with the help of our son Taylor, was busy shuffling travel trailers and heavy equipment around to allow access for fire trucks, but I told him where I'd be and gave him a kiss goodbye.

From the parking lot of the facility where I dropped Dad, I observed a massive mushroom cloud—that looked more like an explosion—in the sky directly above where the fire was burning near our property. I had no idea if Matt and Taylor had left yet, but hoped they'd beat me to the marina; however, they didn't. In utter shock, I sat perched on our boat's vinyl couch, watching the Wall Fire's bright red glow and waiting to hear from Matt... four very long hours. Through spotty cell phone reception, my adrenalized husband explained, "We stayed as long as we could, Jenny. The fire was raging right at the back of the shop, then I saw the smoke rise up and turn into a tornado or something! It got really dark out, and the fire started to surround us. Taylor and I got out of there while we still could." He paused briefly, then his voice cracked, "I think it's gone." He was talking about our home, but my family was safe, and that's all I really cared about. Around midnight, we received an update from CalFire: "Your home is still there, but that can change by morning." The fire raged on; Matt and I got almost no sleep.

Four days later, Matt and I returned to our fire-stricken property. Within our blackened seven acres stood our three-bedroom, three-bath, three-level stick-built home, still somehow surrounded by a lovely green lawn. The shop and all equipment and vehicles had been left unharmed as well. I couldn't believe it. I was in further disbelief later that day when I saw the news photo a member of the Associated Press had captured of my husband—*my* fireman—fleeing the fiery scene in his big, black truck that nightmarish evening. That photo became Getty Image #811021836.

As frightening as it was, the Wall Fire paled in comparison to the following year's Camp Fire. Sparking on eleven-eight-eighteen, the deadliest and most destructive wildfire in California's history razed all of Concow—my old stomping ground—and, among other communities, the entire town of Paradise. In total, there were eighty-six fatalities (not including three people unaccounted for), eighteen thousand plus structures lost, and more than a hundred fifty thousand acres burned.

ACKNOWLEDGMENTS

From the first smoke rings ever forward, I'd like to thank my late mother, Bobbi. Thank you, Mom, for giving me my heart. You never knew it, but mine is a direct reflection of yours. I hope you're doing well on the other side. I love you, and I'll see you again someday.

Curt Pesman, at the beginning of my project your words verbatim: "I'm helping you because you're writing your ass off." From your initial review of the manuscript in 2013 to your final revisions of the pre-published book in 2018, all to ensure my story was well told, you never threw in the towel. I have no idea how I can ever fully repay you, but for now I wish to give you a huge *thank you*.

Alice Peck, thank you for your thoughtful story development and careful edits; you helped make *Smoke Rings Rising* the best it could be.

And, Duane Stapp, great job on the interior design and cover!

I'd like to thank Lisa Frederickson of breakingthecycles. com, Dawn Clancy of Growing Up Chaotic, and Michael King of Facing Addiction for seeing the importance of my story when it seemed nobody would listen. Also, Mental Health America and

National Association of Drug Endangered Children, thank you for giving me the opportunity to present at your conferences.

Tim Harlan, Ph.D., your countless cups of freshly brewed coffee, boatload of tissue, your unique ability to reel me in when I needed it, and unwavering support have made me a better person. Since the beginning of our time together, you have always left the door open for me when it would have been much, much easier for you to, in fact, show the door to me instead. Tim, you're a trouper. Thank you for standing in my corner.

To my sons and stepsons, being a parent has been the greatest gift in my life—thank you for being the remarkable men that you are. A special shout out to Zack and Tony: thank you both for supporting my story even though much of what I was writing was painful for you to think about. In time, I hope this book is as healing for you as it was for me.

Matt, my amazing husband, thank you for your grounded commitment to me and our family. Were it not for your steadfast love and support, I wouldn't have found the courage to delve into the darkest parts of my soul and expose it in *Smoke Rings Rising* for the whole world to read. Know I hold you in the highest regard, Matt. And thank you for loving *all* of me.

ABOUT THE AUTHOR

Jennifer Hunt has been employed as a court reporter for more than twenty years. Born in French Camp, CA, Hunt lived in nearby Stockton until the age of 13, when her family moved to Oroville, Butte County, CA, where she currently resides and works. A happily married mother of two and stepmother of three, she enjoys writing, reading, and traveling to beautiful places with her family.

Hunt's commissioned articles have appeared in such popular websites as Growing up Chaotic, Facing Addiction, and Breakingthecycles.com.

To date, she has presented at the annual conferences of the National Association of Drug Endangered Children in Reno, NV, and Mental Health America in Washington, D.C.

jenniferlhunt.com
Twitter: @jennhuntsrr
Facebook: smoke.rings.rising.

CPSIA information can be obtained
at www.ICGtesting.com
Printed in the USA
LVHW111603061119
636549LV00005B/941/P